IMAGES
of America

AROUND
BURNT HILLS

D1410854

Reflections by Michele Venezio.

For generations, the Mohawk Indians roamed the land of Ballston, treasuring the clear streams, the lake, deep forests, and vegetation. Some claim they still have Native American spirits in their homes on Shanantaha, the Mohawk name for Ballston Lake.

IMAGES
of America

AROUND
BURNT HILLS

Katherine Q. Briaddy

ARCADIA

Published by Arcadia Publishing,
an imprint of Tempus Publishing, Inc.
2 Cumberland Street
Charleston, SC 29401

Printed in Great Britain.

Library of Congress Catalog Card Number: 98-86606

For all general information contact Arcadia Publishing at:
Telephone 843-853-2070
Fax 843-853-0044
E-Mail arcadia@charleston.net

For customer service and orders:
Toll-Free 1-888-313-BOOK

Visit us on the internet at http://www.arcadiaimages.com

Dedication

We, the senior class of 1948, take pride in dedicating our yearbook to
r advisor, Mrs. Mary E. Quellhorst.
You have provided us with:
   A better understanding of our fellowmen,
You have placed a goal for us:
   A patient and intelligent citizen in an intricate world,
You shall always be remembered by us for:
   Your understanding and righteousness of our individual differences,
   Because that's the way you are.

Fifty years later, I have the honor of dedicating this book to the same lady who taught at Burnt Hills-Ballston Lake Central School from 1942 until 1962. She was my mentor, my true friend, and my Mom.

CONTENTS

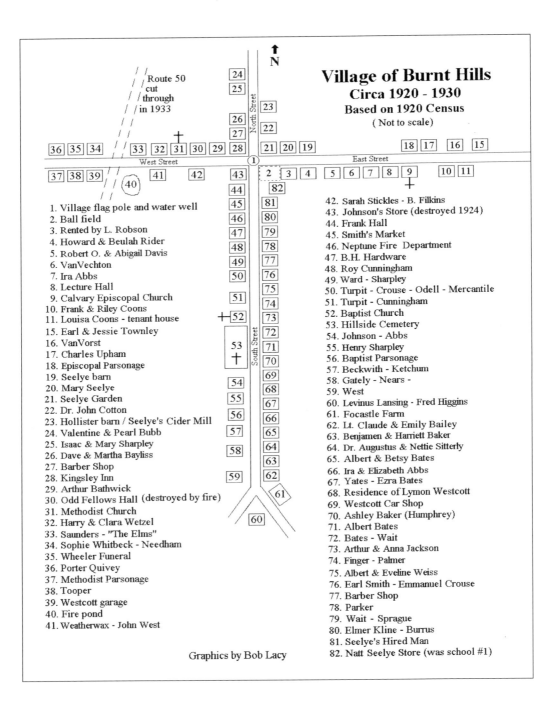

Graphics by Bob Lacy

INTRODUCTION

Burnt Hills is a hamlet in the town of Ballston, and it derives its name from the Mohawk Indian practice of burning fields. The ensuing new growth would entice deer and other game for an easy kill. For generations, the Mohawks had traveled to their favorite hunting ground in Ballston. Twice a year, they paddled their canoes from their long houses near Amsterdam, down the Mohawk River to the Alplaus Creek. They portaged their boats to their beloved Shanantaha, now known as Ballston Lake.

The mineral springs to the north were cherished for their healing powers. They were considered a gift from the Great Spirit. The ill and the elderly were taken to the springs. Those who did not recover were buried on the high bank that runs on the east side of Shanantaha.

One generation later, the descendants of these Mohawks would return to Shanantaha to butcher, not deer, but American patriots. After all, these men had taken the Mohawks' land and built houses on their sacred burial grounds. Rev. Eliphalet Ball and his followers were settling in the town of Ballston in the early 1770s. During the American Revolution in 1780, the Mohawks returned with the British to burn and loot the houses on the northern portion of Middle Lane Road. The American patriots who lived there were captured and imprisoned in Canada.

Ballston was a closely knit community, and many of the founding families intermarried. Morehouses married into the Merchant family, which married into the Raymond family. Van Vrankens married into the Whitbeck family, which married into the Weed family, which married into the Jennings family, which married into the Abbs family. The Waterman family married into the Curtis family, which married into the Larkin family, which married into the Wheeler family, which married into the Tibbets family. If a family reunion was held in 1900, half the town would attend. It was much more likely for those who lived close to each other to marry than to wed one from another town or county.

This book is based on photographs and letters found in an old trunk in the attic of the house at 97 Lakehill Road. The trunk was filled with moth-eaten clothing, dusty canceled check books, and hundreds of yellowed photographs, mostly unidentified. Tucked in the bottom right corner were 50 letters, tied in a faded, pink ribbon.

The letters were written by Frank Coons to his wife-to-be, Edna Davis. Frank wrote his letters from Burnt Hills, New York, to Edna in Columbus, Ohio. They were obviously leery of the gossip going around Burnt Hills concerning them. The first letter was written in 1926, and the last was written just before their marriage in 1931. At the time of their marriage, the bride was 53 years old, and the groom was 68. Since Frank was aware of the gossip, all of his letters were mailed from Schenectady, Scotia, or Ballston Spa, rather than the local post office in Ballston Lake or Burnt Hills. At one point, Frank was spotted in the Schenectady train station boarding a train going west. He was on his way to visit Edna, but had told his neighbors he was going to Florida. When he returned home, the gossip over his trip was nearly unbearable to him.

There are some recurring themes in the letters. Frank repeatedly tries to convince Edna that he is still strong and healthy. He also tries to convince her of his generosity, especially after she called him a "tightwad." Frank frets over the possibility that Edna will gain weight, while she corrects his spelling, she being much more educated than he. She is more in tuned to the social graces of the day. And while they are concerned over the gossip about themselves, they did not hesitate to engage in it over their neighbors. The letters have been edited, and photographs have been chosen to coincide with each letter.

The letters provide a unique look into life in Burnt Hills 70 years ago. The 1920s were years of amazing vitality. They were really the formative years of modern American society. There was a huge technological development and the rise of a new type of industrial economy, typified by mass production and mass consumption. There was a breakdown of old habits and patterns of thought, which prepared the way for the future. Societies do not give up old ideals and attitudes easily. The conflicts between the older elements of traditional American culture and the prophets of the new day were as bitter as they were extensive. Such matters as religion, marriage, and moral standards, as well as issues over race, prohibition, and immigration, were at the heart of the conflict. So step back in time, when the automobile was a new mode of transportation, women were finding their own identity, the radio was uniting the world, the stock market was booming, people indulged in luxuries paid for in credit, and stamps were only 2¢.

Acknowledgments

A sincere thank you is extended to the following people for their assistance and generosity in loaning photographs: Roy Arnold, Rachael Clothier, Robert Speck, Nancy Voehringer, Bunny and John Guyer, Catherine Shorey, Richard Wilkinson, Don Feeney, Genevieve VanPatten, Bruce Armer, Anna Thorpe, Robert Lacy, Jackie Mosher, Shirley and Harry Davis, D. Ward and his grandfather, Jerry Williams, Ginny Whitten, Loris Sawchuk, Pat Merriam, Reverend Beth Dewey, Dot Hopkinson, Bob Boice, Phyllis Brandt, Ben Heckman, George Yager, Irena Wooten, Lucy Doriguizzi, Phyllis and George Schulze, Ruth Mead, Connie Falconer, Bob McBroom, Ruth Roerig, Chester Jennings, Merrill McCall, Pete Sarto, Bill and Mary Egan, Lawrence Townley, Florence Breitbeck, Myra Kinns Headley, Terry Morris, Bernice Knight, Lewis Schumacher, Art Mengel, and Anita Wagner. The illustrations on each chapter heading page were drawn by Helen Moore Sewell, a noted New York City artist. She was a frequent visitor to Burnt Hills and the niece of Emily Moore Bailey. The artistic work of Michele Venezio, Edward Sutphen, and George Shorey has been invaluable. Finally, and most importantly, thanks go to Marie Cunningham, who discovered the trunk, recognized its historic value, and donated it.

One
THE BRIDE'S FAMILY

The bride, Edna Davis, and the groom, Frank Coons, pose for a photograph in 1935.

THE BRIDE'S FAMILY TREE

The receiver of the following letters was Edna Davis. The Davis family genealogy can be traced back to 1612 in England. Edna Davis's ancestor was Dr. Samuel Davis, who was born in 1765 and came to Ballston in 1790. He provided medical care for the founding families for 50 years. He married Mary Kirby Dunham in 1789, and they settled at 151 Middle Line Road. Dr. Davis died in 1840, and his wife died in 1855. They are buried in the family plot in Briggs Cemetery.

Their son Henry married Abby Raymond in 1828, and the son of Henry and Abby, Robert Oliphant Davis, married Abbie McMullen in 1866. Robert and Abbie were the parents of Samuel (b. 1869), Louis (b. 1871), Edna (b. 1878), Robert (b. 1884), and Mary (b. 1888). These children were baptized at Saint Paul's Episcopal Church in Charlton. Edna's two older siblings died before she was born. They died within five days of each other in January 1876, possibly of some childhood contagious disease, such as the measles. Their father died in 1920, and their mother died in 1930 of myocarditis due to the "grip." Edna was educated at Syracuse University and became a librarian at Ohio State University in Columbus, Ohio.

Edna's brother Robert married Edith Deforest. They were the parents of Robert (b. 1912), Edith (b. 1918), Frances (b. 1919), Margaret (b. 1920), and Harry (b. 1922). Harry and his wife, Shirley Witbeck, reside at the family homestead on Charlton Road.

Edna Davis Coons died January 17, 1959, at the age of 81. A plaque at Calvary Episcopal Church pays tribute to her leadership in Saint Mary's Guild there.

Edna Eva Davis was born in 1878, the daughter of Robert O. Davis and Abbie McMullen. At age three, she had her picture taken by Jesse Wooley, a noted Ballston Spa photographer.

The childhood home of Edna Davis is located at 310 Charlton Road. Edna's father, Robert Davis, raised fine Holstein cows. In fact, her husband-to-be often bought cows from the Davis farm. Harry and Shirley Witbeck Davis currently run the Mourning Kill Bake Shop there. His grandfather, Robert O. Davis, moved his family to this house *c*. 1866, when he sold the Samuel Davis house to Austin Slade.

Robert O. Davis (seated) was born in 1858. He poses with his son, Robert A. Davis, born 1884; and grandson, Robert, who was born in 1912.

Mary Davis was Edna's sister. Mary died in 1928 at the age of 40. The cause of death was "embolism due to the removal of tonsils." The Davis family was opposed to Edna's marriage to Frank.

Mary Davis, the daughter of Henry Davis and Abby Raymond, was born in 1847. She poses in a gown similar to those worn during the Civil War period.

The home of Dr. Samuel Davis is located at 151 Middle Line Road. He came to Ballston in 1790 and practiced medicine until his death in 1840. He and his wife, Mary Kirby, were the parents of John (b. 1792), Samuel (b. 1793), Abigail (b. 1795), Henry (b. 1798), and Melissa (b. 1804). Henry was Edna's grandfather.

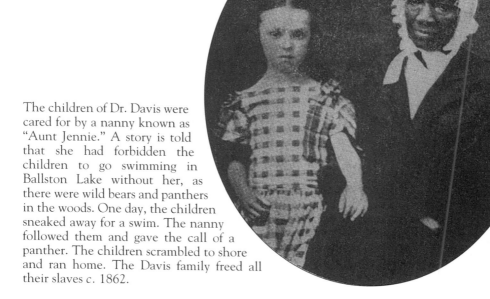

The children of Dr. Davis were cared for by a nanny known as "Aunt Jennie." A story is told that she had forbidden the children to go swimming in Ballston Lake without her, as there were wild bears and panthers in the woods. One day, the children sneaked away for a swim. The nanny followed them and gave the call of a panther. The children scrambled to shore and ran home. The Davis family freed all their slaves c. 1862.

Robert O. and Abigail Davis purchased property for this house at 97 Lakehill Road in 1914 from Nathan Seelye. When Robert Davis dismantled his cheese factory, which was on the Mourningkill Creek, some of the lumber was used to construct this house. Abigail willed the house to Edna in 1930. Edna and Frank Coons lived here after their marriage.

From left to right, Shirley Witbeck Davis, Harry Davis, Ruth Merchant Center, and Glen Center unveil the New York State History Marker at the Dr. Samuel Davis house in 1996. Harry Davis is Edna's nephew. The Centers owned the Sam Davis house for years. While renovating, a secret room was uncovered, leading to the belief that the house was a stop, or "hold," on the Underground Railroad.

Two

THE GROOM'S FAMILY

This photograph of Frank Coons was taken during his term in office as town supervisor from 1908 to 1909. He ran on the Democratic ticket.

F. B. COONS

The Groom's Family Tree

Frank Burton Coons was the grandson of Solymon Coons, who was born in Sand Lake in 1805, the son of John and Lucy Coons. Solymon was first married to Martha Burton. Their children were named Solymon, Julia, William, Jefferson, Harriet, and Anna. After Martha died in 1854, Solymon married Louisa Hamilton, a descendant of Alexander Hamilton. They were the parents of John and Frank. Frank was born in 1863 when the Coons family resided on Middle Line Road on a farm formerly owned by General James Gordon, of Revolutionary War fame. Coincidentally, Alexander Hamilton was with General George Washington when they visited this farm-estate in 1783. By 1870, the Solymon Coons family had moved to what is now Lakehill Road. Solymon died in 1891, at the age of 85. He is buried in the family plot of the Calvary Episcopal Church cemetery with his wives. Louisa died in 1920.

Frank first married Maria Crippen, the daughter of Riley Crippen and Sarah Betts. Their son, born in 1890, was named Riley Hamilton. Riley married Amelia DeRouville. They were the parents of Dorothy, Frank, and twins, John and George.

Maria, Frank Coons's first wife, became mentally ill in 1919 and was committed to Utica State Hospital until her death in 1925. After her death, Frank courted Edna Davis until their marriage in 1931. He was 68 years old, and she was 53. They had 14 years together until Frank's death in 1945. He died, apparently at home, from "myocardia due to old age," having spent his entire adult life within one block in Burnt Hills. He rests within the same bounds.

Frank Coons was born on the Maplewood Stock Farm. His father lived there at that time, according to the 1860 census. His property was worth $10,000 and his personal worth was $4,000. The house was located at 217 Middle Line Road. It was originally owned by General James Gordon.

Solymon Coons, Frank's father, was born in 1805 and died in 1891. He owned huge tracks of land in Ballston. In 1881, he sold 78 acres of land to his sons, Frank and John. The land was east of the Episcopal church on the southside of Lakehill Road. This photograph is labeled "Solymon Coons and his wife."

By 1870, Solymon and Louisa were settled on Lakehill Road. At that time, Frank was seven years old and attending school, probably at District #1 on Kingsley Road. The house is located at 73 Lakehill Road.

In March of 1914, Louisa Coons was given a surprise 90th birthday party at her home. She was a graduate of Emma Willand School with highest honors in 1846. At the time of her party, she was described as a "remarkably well-preserved old lady, who keeps apace with current affairs by reading." Her house is at 69 Lakehill Road.

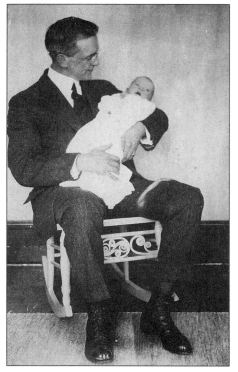

Riley Coons, Frank's son, was born in 1890. After Maria Coons, Riley's mother, was committed to Utica State Hospital, Riley moved his young family into his father's house. Riley assisted his father with running the farm and their milk business.

Three
1926

Mrs. Bubb lived on Scotch Bush Road and made rag rugs. She was the mother of Vallie Bubb and grandmother of Bernice Knight, a life-long resident of Burnt Hills.

Burnt Hills, New York
Oct. 19, 1926

My dear Miss Davis,

Another wet Sunday forenoon like last Sunday, but it is clearing now, so that we can go out with the car for a short ride.

Your letters are certainly very interesting, and I am wondering what I can write that will be of interest to you. Our environments are so much different; you are living in the midst of so many various activities that you have something new each line you write; while with me it is more of the sameness from day to day. I might tell you about the crops how good they are or how poor and of the cows, hens and pigs, what income we expect to receive, how high the taxes are and what hard times farmers have to make ends meet. If I judge you rightly, I don't think that line of talk would appeal to you although you were from a farm family.

I thought at one time I might have the classification of a gentleman farmer, as that puts one on a higher plane, but the way we have been working for the past month it has set me back to a plain farmer, and I have enjoyed the work, also it helps me forget for a time the lonesome feeling that comes after a period of pleasant enjoyment.

I have not read any new books lately, have so many magazines and papers to read. Will take up books and plays later in the season and go to Proctors. My recreation consists of doing cross-word puzzles and listening to the loud speaker. I am also quite regular in my attendance at Rotary.

In my last letter, I mentioned the gossip that we are responsible for. Do not worry. If you think these letters are too formal, just let down a bar and get in the broad field of informality. Perhaps they would be more spicy to read, but not wise, so forget this last part.

Sincerely yours,

F.B. Coons

Author's note—The loud speaker was an early term for the radio. WGY came on the air in 1922, and favorite programs were *Amos and Andy* and *The Shadow*.

Tourists stopped at the village well to get water for their cars. The well never ran dry. This 1913 Buick touring car has the top folded down. The spare tire is on the fender.

This photograph was taken looking north on Kingsley Road. Johnson's Store is on the left and the Hollister/Cotton house is the white one on the right. The village flagpole can be seen in the intersection of what is now Kingsley and Lakehill Road. It was standing in 1935.

Johnson's Store was established in 1780, one of the oldest landmarks in Burnt Hills. Canned food and fresh food was sold, as well as clothing and household items. Townsfolk voted there, got their mail (and gossip) there, and gathered for the Fourth of July celebrations there. The store was built by William Kingsley, who also built a hotel to accommodate farmers driving their herds from Schenectady to Saratoga. When the store burned in 1924, it was run by Nathan Seelye.

October 31, 1926

My dear Edna,

That drops one bar and is not so formal whether it is proper or not. I can do it easier than you as I have the advantage of age.

I was not going to write because I was worried that I might have said something in my last letter to offend you, particularly the latter part. You might have thought that I said something improper or not becoming a gentleman. What I meant to say was that I thought we both had been rather careful how we expressed ourselves, a little different than when we were talking to each other.

It has rained again on Sunday, so we stay home without riding in the car— saves gas and tires, but I would much prefer to take a ride. This is a quiet day in Burnt Hills. Mr. Upham stopped by for a brief visit. He always livens things up with his freshest update of the local gossip.

We just had one young married teacher resign, and I happened to be the one she informed. We have to secure a teacher in her place. Did not have much to choose from— five applicants, three were from the Catholic denomination and two elderly ladies. I fear some of them are Irish. We selected one of the young ones. What is your opinion in regard to age and religion provided they have the same qualifications?

Was down to Schenectady yesterday and saw Mr. Bailey. You may remember me talking about him. We are in the wholesale food business together. Anyway, he asked where I had been as he missed me. I told him that I had been busy and he said that the trip to Manchester, Vermont, must have put new life into me, so you see that eventful ride does not die out, even among those who were not in the party.

I don't suppose you gave it a thought that today is my birthday. Amelia had a birthday cake in my honor with candles on it (not the full amount). If I told you how old I am, you might want to put back those bars you let down a week ago, but any time you really care to know, I will tell you the truth.

Shall I write more or not? I am somewhat wary of my closing thoughts as I might bungle them. What I was going to say is that while we have known of each other for a long time, still we have met only a few times and that was last August and then not alone. Now, we are carrying on a regular correspondence. What name do you give it? You are more versed in such matters.

Just nicely got started and now I have to close for lack of space, so I will say good-night.

F.B.C.

Charles Upham stands on his porch at 82 Lakehill Road. He came to Burnt Hills in 1877 and served as Ballston's town clerk for 17 years.

Seelye's barn is pictured on the north side of Lakehill Road, facing south. The Seelye farm consisted of 200 acres. The barn was located near the driveway leading to the BH-BL High School. A street lamp can be seen on the left by the sidewalk.

November 11, 1926

My dear Edna,

You know what I thought after reading your last letter? That there was a lonesome girl in Columbus the night she wrote those lines. I am awfully sorry if I disappointed you in not attending the football game, as I would much rather have gone there than any other place, and it was gratifying to know that I would have been welcomed.

You understand that it is a busy time of the year getting things secured before cold weather sets in and laborers hard to get. Before I forget, I want to thank you for the birthday card. It was thoughtful of you.

Today I have been celebrating Armistice Day. Started out rather early for Schenectady this morning, met several of my friends, and then had lunch at the Van Curler with the Rotarians, heard a good talk even though it was a woman speaker. Spent the day by going to Proctors. Arrived home at 6 o'clock and attended a card party at the schoolhouse given by the PTA. The best of all is that I had the highest score and won a pair of socks for my skill. They are not quite to my taste, but will come in handy when I discard others in need of mending, although I am good with a needle.

Thursday we had a good speaker on American relations in Europe. He carries to the idea that we should support the League of Nations and that we must do whatever necessary to avoid another world war like the last one we have been through.

Have a heart. You keep asking for more pages. I have never written letters like this before.

I find that I have to answer some questions from your last letter. You omitted two stages, the first is the "puppy" stage confined to the young and the last is called what President Coolidge calls the "blissful" stage. The next question was about your stationery and you changed partly on account of my family. You know I don't think they have caught onto it yet, at least they have not said anything. If your last letter had come Tuesday, Amelia would have brought it from the post office, and then I would have been questioned. Do send me some of those impulsive letters of yours. I am curious to know what they are like.

In order to have something in reserve for the next time, I will close.

Sincerely yours,

F.B.C.

During World War I, the soldiers from Ballston served in the 27th Field Artillery. They fought in France, and those at home suffered exceptionally harsh winters. There was an earthquake in Burnt Hills in 1916. The end of the war was celebrated on Armistice Day, November 11, 1918. It is now called Veteran's Day.

LIVING INSIGNI
of the
TWENTY-SEVENTH DIVISIC
"NEW YORK'S OWN"

These young men, Bill Quellhorst (left) and Tom Clancy, were to fight in World War II just 15 years after Frank wrote this letter, warning against the possibility of another "world war like the last one we have been through."

My dear Edna,

How would you take it is I should write one of those "mushy" letters? Now, my being a novice at the game I might not do it justice, so I feel much safer to keep along the same lines as formerly, and it might embarrass you to follow suit as you said you would do, although you had more experience than I.

Now you are positive that I am a cold disposition as you expected to hear something interesting and perhaps pleasing, sorry to disappoint you. Your opinion would change if you knew me better or could see me instead of being 600 miles away.

I presume Thanksgiving is very lonely for you unless you have the pleasure of being with some friends, and then it is not like being with your own people. On the other hand, think of the pleasure you derive from being in a large city, holding a fine position and earning a large salary and mingling with those cultured people. I spent the day quietly and then went for a ride.

In regard to my trips south, I have been there four times, once I went alone and I can assure you it was mighty lonesome. The last two winters a gentleman friend went with me. I am surprised that you would even think that it could have been a lady companion. I steered clear of all females down there, that is doing better than some men would have done, don't you think so knowing them as well as you do.

Just got back from calling on the Cruickshanks.

Gilbert Seelye has a new car. I have not seen him out in it yet. Betty has probably ridden in it.

I stopped and called on your sister, Mary, yesterday morning but seeing Antoinette going in the door, I was immediately timid and did not go in, might start something new again.

After I release one of these ordinary letters I fear that I have said something I ought not to have said and worry until I get your reply, then I feel easier. You don't have to worry about yours for they are always alright.

Sincerely yours,

Frank

Mr. W. Cruickshank, principal of the BH-BL school, lived at 120 Lakehill Road. Mrs. Needham made and sold fancy hats from her parlor at this house. It was later owned by the Witbeck family. The Wheeler funeral home was next door.

The Weatherwax Hotel and Saloon was located at 113 Lakehill Road. It was known as a "pretty rough place." The John West family later lived there. He was a machinist in the "electric factory," i.e. General Electric.

At the corner of what is now Route 50 and Lakehill Road, the Saunders Mansion stood. In 1965, it was moved up the embankment to make way for a gas station. The mansion, known as "The Elms," was built by a Revolutionary War soldier, Stephen Clark. It was sold to Dr. Henry Saunders, who was the father of four sons and four daughters. All the girls were married in the house, the first in 1838. This photograph was taken on the eve of the house moving.

My dear Edna,

Snow and plenty of it for the time of the year. Poets and others say beautiful snow, but I don't care for it. Only a few years ago it was considered quite a treat to have your cutter or sleigh ready for the coming of the snow and have the first sleigh ride of the season but now that is all changed and not many avail themselves of that pleasure. Automobiles have superseded the sleigh where the roads are cleared, and we progress along. That reminds me, when you are home for the holidays if the weather or roads will permit perhaps we can take another ride if it is agreeable to you. We cannot expect to have as pleasant a trip as we had the last time but we may be able to get in a short ride and have dinner if nothing more.

I won't drop you as Wilson did and I hope you will not do the same by me. Let me down easy so I can survive the shock.

Do you read the Saturday Evening Post? I presume your reading consists of a much higher type. Perhaps mine would be if I had so many books to choose from. Dorothy thinks now that she will become a librarian.

Too late now for Columbus as you will be coming home next week, but if I do later on, my folks will know where I am going. No strings on me yet, the public may not know, and I will truthfully say I would rather see Columbus than any other city. How does that please you?

We have had some very interesting speakers at Rotary and plan on raising $1000 for crippled children. About my going to Florida, if I do it won't be until February. That was a very good suggestion of yours to go your way.

Have you got your Christmas presents bought and made. If I remember you were going to make me one. I have my cards, given to all that I have been asked in the way of charity. Will send my brother and his wife a check and then I am done except one for you. Your informer said that was allowable but restricted me so I will have to get more advice.

What day of the week do you arrive here? I thought it would be Friday, the 24th on the 11:20 train due in Schenectady. If nothing prevents I will meet you, and we will go out for lunch and have a visit by ourselves before you go home. Tell your people the train may be late and not to expect you until later in the day.

This is no masterpiece, but I don't see how I can do better. I suppose I could get more appropriate stationery.

Sincerely,

Frank

A sleigh is being pulled in front of the Seelye home c. 1910. According to the family Bible, Nathan Alson Seelye married Mary Susan Thompson in 1868. Their children were named Jennie, Marie Antoinette, James, Gilbert, Susan, and Nathan. They lived at 96 Lakehill Road.

A postman poses on Lakehill Road. The Kingsley Inn and barn is pictured in the background. Mail was transported by steam train to Ballston Lake. Porter Quivey ran a stagecoach and delivered the mail from Ballston Lake to Johnson's Store/Post Office in Burnt Hills.

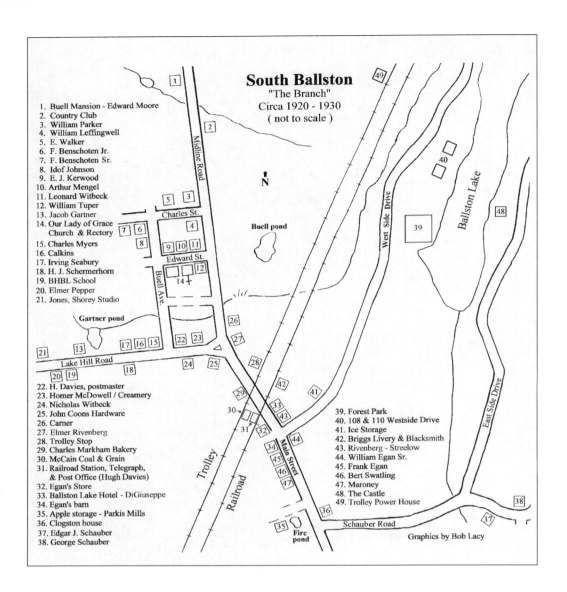

South Ballston
"The Branch"
Circa 1920 - 1930
(not to scale)

1. Buell Mansion - Edward Moore
2. Country Club
3. William Parker
4. William Leffingwell
5. E. Walker
6. F. Benschoten Jr.
7. F. Benschoten Sr.
8. Idof Johnson
9. E. J. Kerwood
10. Arthur Mengel
11. Leonard Witbeck
12. William Tuper
13. Jacob Gartner
14. Our Lady of Grace
    Church & Rectory
15. Charles Myers
16. Calkins
17. Irving Seabury
18. H. J. Schermerhorn
19. BHBL School
20. Elmer Pepper
21. Jones, Shorey Studio

22. H. Davies, postmaster
23. Homer McDowell / Creamery
24. Nicholas Witbeck
25. John Coons Hardware
26. Carner
27. Elmer Rivenberg
28. Trolley Stop
29. Charles Markham Bakery
30. McCain Coal & Grain
31. Railroad Station, Telegraph,
    & Post Office (Hugh Davies)
32. Egan's Store
33. Ballston Lake Hotel - DiGiuseppe
34. Egan's barn
35. Apple storage - Parkis Mills
36. Clogston house
37. Edgar J. Schauber
38. George Schauber

39. Forest Park
40. 108 & 110 Westside Drive
41. Ice Storage
42. Briggs Livery & Blacksmith
43. Rivenberg - Streelow
44. William Egan Sr.
45. Frank Egan
46. Bert Swatling
47. Maroney
48. The Castle
49. Trolley Power House

Graphics by Bob Lacy

Four

1927

Mrs. Needham made and sold fancy
hats from her Burnt Hills home at 120
Lake Hill Road.

My dear Edna,

You seemed to have been out of luck this trip home coming and going, getting into Schenectady four hours late when you had a nice young man waiting to take you to lunch, then icy walks so it was a question who would fall first, then ride up in the bus with same man so that the whole community was talking about it and still talking, returning another long wait in the station, but part of that time was well spent—I hope as enjoyable to you as it was to me.

Mr. Upham has started going again, four times to Saratoga last week attending the crusader meetings of your church. This week he has Mrs. Ellsworth meet him in Schenectady and then takes her to Proctors. I wonder if they will be talked about as much as some other couple that went there.

Well I attended the stock holders meeting at the Van Curler, and you should have seen me when I am dressed up-looked pretty as a picture and was about as long dressing as a woman. There were about 200 present with their wives, a male quartet, two speakers and good eats. It was quite an affair.

Last week I went to two chicken suppers and had chicken for Sunday dinner. I don't care for any this week. The Country Club supper netted $900, and the church supper raised $350. You may think I bought two tickets to these places, but I went alone as usual and caused no remarks.

It is difficult to turn a good profit from farming, between grain and hardware costs and farm labor. The same man, George Young, stays with me on the farm for another year so I have that settled, expect I will have to assist him as usual, although I pay him $80 a month for his labor.

I trust I did not embarrass you for the little entertainment I gave you. I thought you appreciated it though in fact, I know so.

Sincerely yours,

F.B. Coons

The Burnt Hills Hardware Store was owned by Roy Cunningham. It was an outgrowth of a blacksmith shop owned by Frank Hall.

The Kingsley Inn, its horse sheds, and Bayliss's Barber Shop (pictured under the tree) were located on the northwest corner of the Burnt Hills intersection. Earl Bayliss was a barber and repairer of fine clocks. He claimed to have fixed a clock that belonged to General Burgoyne and was passed to General Gates at the surrender. The barber shop was a gathering place where home remedies and gossip were shared. It was open until 2 a.m. on Saturdays.

The 1920s were an era of "wonderful nonsense." A country club was built at 50 Midline Road. Membership consisted of prominent people who were voted in by secret ballot. Dinners, games of chance, and dancing to the music of the "Melody Girls" orchestra were held in the large ballroom. Flappers did the Charleston. A golf course was planned, but never completed due to the Depression. Alvah Smith converted the building into apartments when the club folded in the 1930s.

Burnt Hills, NY
January 29, 1927

My dear Edna,

I have never been so short of ammunition as I am this time, been to no plays, have not read any books, nor taken any married woman to the Sunday movie. It is a quiet, rather monotonous way of life.

Twenty below zero Thursday and now thawing. From what I read in the papers I don't know if it would be safe to travel along the Ohio River. I might get marooned, which would not be too bad if I had pleasant company to pass the time with.

It is no wonder there are so many heavy weights out there. The women have the best of food. You have got the wrong opinion about my liking to see them as large and plump as you talk about, from 125 to 150 pounds will do nicely if one is tall enough to carry that much.

I don't hear anything about Gilbert and Betty. Do you? Only that she picked out the ring herself, she to get one to her liking, don't know when the event is to take place or what Antoinette is to do, don't imagine she will stay there.

Are you interested very much in evolution? I understand most of the professors and scientific men believe in it. The Reverends do not. They say it is all theory and they have not proven much. I don't believe in it myself, especially the ape part. Why haven't they improved with the rest of us?

I have my income report filled out. Perhaps I would be richer if I got rid of some of this property. One could travel, even go to Italy. Your rich relative must be spending money on his young wife, that is the one who married the nurse.

You know you have given me several cordial invitations to visit Columbus on my way to Florida. If you do not hear otherwise, I will leave Schenectady Friday night Feb. 11th on the 6:35 train, the one you always take and make your friendly weekend visit. I have told no one that I was going a different route or even that I was going to Florida for sure this winter.

I remain most sincerely yours,

F.B.C.

Betty (Elsie) Bogert married Gilbert Seelye on April 9, 1928. They met when her father, Rev. Henry Bogert, was hit by a car near Johnson's store. Gilbert was a state senator for 22 years, a charter member of the Burnt Hills Fire Department, and a member of the board of education.

Nathan Seelye (left) poses with his brother Gilbert inside Johnson's Store. The post office boxes are on the right-hand wall. The flag that was raised and lowered daily at the flagpole was kept here.

New Port Richey, Florida
February 16, 1927

My dear Edna,

I arrived here yesterday morning. The people in my car were very congenial and easy to talk to. One very good-looking young man was a Rotarian and well informed, a middle-aged Priest—broad minded and unusually good company, a professor from Amherst and one or two other men.

The bus was not running, so I was obliged to hire a taxi. Arrived at my brother's and was surprised to learn that Mary had been ill with the asthma for nearly a month, so I am stopping at the hotel. The weather here is ideal, wear summer apparel. Still wear my homely shoes that give comfort to my feet as I have no others to wear. Travel is so much easier here this time of year, compared to home.

Well, any gossip or sensation? It would take a better and more attractive fellow than I to even make an impression among your friends. What did Mr. and Mrs. B have to say? I surely had a good time in Columbus.

FBC

This view is on Lakehill Road facing east. The Frank Coons house is on the right. Jesse Townley led a campaign to save the trees when the road was paved.

There were times when Lakehill Road was only good for sledding, certainly not for driving a car.

According to a newspaper account, Frank Coons owned the car in the ditch when it was in an accident at the intersection of Lakehill Road and Main Street. It was run off the road by another car in 1914. In the photograph, a sign can be seen. It reads, "Buell Heights, Building Lots for Sale." The sign was on the future site of the Ballston Lake Post Office. G. Briggs lived in the house at the right, and the house at 6 Midline is on the left.

My dear Edna,

I arrived here yesterday. I hired a relative of mine through marriage to bring me over in his car from Port Richey, a distance of about 50 miles. His wife, little girl and John and Mary came with us. I did it more to my brother and sister-in-law a ride and to let them see the city and the stores. She wanted to see the stores like all women even if she doesn't buy.

It was a quiet time there. I spent most of my time with them and they were pleased to see me, so you can see I am a favorite. Mary is the only one I consult with in the family in regard to personal matters. I told her about my visit to you in Ohio, but John does not know. I also wanted to know how they were fixed financially. Since the real estate boom, he has invested heavily, more than he should have, so I don't know what the outcome will be. While there I had the pleasure of going by motor boat up the river. It is a narrow, deep stream and flows into the Gulf. I offered a young man a cigarette. A young woman accepted one too. It was the first woman I ever saw smoke and I hope it will be the last.

I have a ticket and reservation to leave here on Sunday and expect to reach home on Tuesday night. I look forward to seeing my people, but not the winter weather in Burnt Hills. It is time to get ready for the upcoming apple season.

I thought my sacrifice during Lent was for a spiritual benefit. If you were to use it for weight reduction, don't think it will do any good under the circumstances. Better to let nature take its course. We all have to submit to age. You are all right the way you are.

Your tight-wad friend,

Frank

Mary Morey married Frank's older brother, John Coons. She was one of eight children born to Mr. and Mrs. William Morey of Burnt Hills. John ran a hardware store, later known as Ketchum's in Ballston Lake.

The apple stand at the southeast corner of Kingsley and Lakehill Road was owned by Connie and Harold "Brick" Falconer. Pictured here from left to right are Joyce Barrett, Helen Yates, and Mary McGarty. The stand was on a vacant field next to Falconer's house. Most villagers fondly recall that it was converted to a manger during the Christmas season. The field was previously the ballpark for the Burnt Hills Social and Athletic Club. Members included E. Bates, F. Johnson, N. Seelye, R. Coons, L. Witbeck, I. Abbs, A. Baker, A. Jackson, and manager C. Stickle.

Another fine apple orchard is owned by the Knight family. The homestead was located at 327 Goode Street. The Clarence and John Russell Knight families lived in this two-family house in 1907. When they moved to Burnt Hills, they had to store their furniture at the Methodist church carriage sheds, as Goode Street was too muddy to travel. The house burned in 1956.

My Dear Miss Davis,
My Dear Edna,

One is formal and the other informal. They say people are more informal now, so if any of our friends and others that are so interested in my affairs and yours have really and truly got to know if I am formal, say yes and informal say likewise. I am starting off in a peculiar way, but I am somewhat wrought up. When I got back I heard about all the gossip that has been going on and it certainly got on my nerves for a few days, but I am calmed down now. This all came about my taking the train out of Schenectady for the West. I have been told that two or three people from the city saw me at that time, so the news spread where I was going to stop, and you know how the story goes and expands and the speculations that go with it.

I would not care personally but it is my folks, and I presume your people, that have to hear all the talk. Wherever Riley and Amelia go, they hear about it. As neither one of the other of us by word or deed have acted only as friends, it seems a pity that we cannot enjoy such friendship without so much ado. You wanted to know what Mary said. She did not see any harm in any way.

Mr. Cruickshank invited me to go to Ballston Center this morning, so I went and staid to Sunday school.

I did not get acquainted with any lone females on my travels, I never do, take my word for it as I am not much of a ladies man.

Amelia has finally got her hair bobbed. She says she likes it better this way.

I hear Mary is coming home next week. I won't even dare to call as there will be "pickets" out to watch to see if I do. Sheet is full, so I will close.

Sincerely your friend,

F.B. Coons

The Ballston Center Presbyterian Church was founded by Rev. Eliphaler Ball in 1775. A house of worship was built on the corner of Middle Line Road and Charlton Road in 1803. It was replaced in 1855. The church burned in 1993 and was rebuilt.

The boys varsity basketball team posed in 1928. Players pictured are, from left to right, as follows: (front row) Ludwig Panek (captain), Ross Cunningham, William Plath, Frank Kavorovic, and Louis Baumgartner; (back row) Leroy Gannon, Clarence Ryder, Stanley Knight, William Clarke (coach), Walter Schultz, Milton Myers, and Floyd Brady.

Young girls got their hair bobbed, cutting it short for the "new age" in the 1920s. The girls of the basketball team followed suit. The team members, from left to right, are as follows: (front row) Sibyl Larkin (captain), Elizabeth Jackson, Lorraine Raino, Dorothy Egan, and Dorothy Johnson; (back row) Marian Hewitt, Anita Egan, Gertrude Rice (coach), Mary Shauber, and Elizabeth Peck.

My dear Edna,

I started a letter to you last Sunday and was not going to say very much about the topic that seems to be of interest to so many, but I have heard a little more on the subject. I will open up the case again. Amelia was up the street the other day and someone was kind enough to tell her that you said it was her who started the talk. Evidently they are not satisfied with what they already have and now want to make trouble between families. When Riley got home, she got pretty worked up over the matter (she has a nervous temperament) she denied the accusation very strongly. She said she knew the party that gave out the report that we are married, and it was done only as a joke. My social visit to you was the cause of so much publicity. I received the greater share of it living here and perhaps by being better known. As you said, younger folks can do what they want and get away with it, but let older folks have a little harmless pleasure, then the gossip starts and often times just lies. "Behold how great matter a little fire kindleth."

So the breaking out of this afresh, has left me keyed up and not feeling well. I did not see Mary at all. I thought I might not be received by her or your mother. Decided I would stop on my way home from church, but Nathan and Gilbert were out in front, so I passed by. Later, on my way up, I saw Mr. Upham and he said she had left. I see she got your garden cleaned up. Seelyes' gardens are especially beautiful this year.

Don't let this letter annoy you. I am sorry that any one with a normal mind would start such a report and then try to excuse it by saying it was a joke.

Sincerely your friend,

F.B. Coons

Mary Susan Seelye, the family matriarch, is the elderly lady on the left. The group stands at the gate to their garden, which was on the northeast corner of Lakehill and Kingsley Roads. Mary Seelye was born in 1839 and she died in 1925. During her lifetime she kept meticulous scrapbooks made of newspaper articles covering local and national events. Accounts of the assassination of President Lincoln and the sinking of the *Titanic* are included.

The stone house at 211 Kingsley had lovely rose gardens, as did the house across the street at 200 Kingsley Road. It was owned by Art and Mary Fingers, professional rose growers. The stone house was owned by wagon-maker Alex Hall. Previously, it was the home of William Kingsley. The date 1785 is burned into a floor beam.

Elsie and Frank Yelverton raised peonies and roses in their gardens at 118 Midline Road. The house was previously owned by Patrick Egan, who immigrated from Ireland in 1846.

My dear Edna,

Did you set your watch ahead at 2 a.m.? The hour that I lost in bed, I will make up next September. I would be pleased to compliment you on your last letter. It certainly shows that the writer has a trained mind.

I am making some needed repairs here and the other house. If it does not bore you I will enumerate. You may wonder where the money is coming from to do so. It is one thing to look prosperous, and another to be so. The house has just been painted. The color is ivory with the blinds and sashes green with the porch roof a lighter green. It is quite attractive. The porch furniture is orange with black trimming. Also a new oak floor in one of the front rooms. Now I suppose it will call for a rug. There is a new china closet with glass doors to open up in the dining room, floor varnished and new paper. Painting inside at both houses and an old rocking chair done over. That should be worth something when it is done. That is enough of my affairs.

How have you done with your Lenten fasting? Did you change any of the eight propositions? Height will remain the same until you are old and bent over. I don't think dieting will shorten you any. You could read the article, "Get Rid of the Fat."

Ice this morning on the bird bath, but nice this afternoon, so we took a ride to Ballston Lake to get some buckwheat. Had a blow out, so that means a new tire.

I have a deal with Mr. Robson to drive my car when we are not using it. I like to go sometimes when it is not convenient for Riley to take me. On our last ride there was no one in the back seat. I prefer to have more company.

I bid you good-night.

Sincerely yours,

F.B. Coons

On his way to Parkis Mills, Frank would pass the Ballston Lake Hotel. It was later called the Clothier Saloon and the DiGiuseppie Barber Shop.

Thomas and Katherine McDonough purchased the establishment now known as Carney's in 1936. Teachers from the school were not allowed to visit taverns, and members of the board of education occasionally checked up on them.

Henry Parkis purchased the Seabury Cider Mill in 1927. He added two huge silos, each capable of holding 700 tons of raw buckwheat. Henry gave local farmers a new International tractor. They would repay him by growing buckwheat. The final product was fine pancake flour.

My dear Edna,

I thought I would break away from writing about myself, but when one has been shut in that is all I have to write. I have been confined to my room for a week due to an attack of bronchitis. Could not read but very little, tried the cards, but nothing doing, no smoking, no appetite and not too much sleep. I am coming along slowly, got up and got dressed today. I wanted this letter ready in case I go to Schenectady tomorrow.

On May 7th, Mr. Goodman, the coach of the basketball team, gave a banquet at the Mohawk Hotel for the boys. Mr. Cruickshank and the Board were invited, also Dr. Sitterly was the Toastmaster. No smoking, no singing, no stories, but lasted until late. We have had a winning season this year. Maybe, someday, we will have a football team too.

Now, you have so much to write about. You must lead a very strenuous life. You can do it better now than ten years from now.

I don't see much as been done to your house. You will have to go some to come up to mine. I will wait and see. Perhaps you can go one better then you will have something to crow about.

I presume Mary will be home soon. Will she go back to the same place next year?

When one shortens a letter, you always have something in reserve for next time, so I am not at the end of my rope.

Sincerely yours,

F.B. Coons

"On a hill stands Alma Mater
In her bright array
Showing forth her mystic knowledge
Clearing life's long way.

Look see there our Alma Mater
She's a guiding light
We shall never have another
Cheer maroon and white."

When the school was constructed in 1916, the stakes were mysteriously moved farther south from the road one night. The ample water supply and front lawns were thus provided. Most believe George Schauber was responsible for the move. This photograph was taken in 1928.

46

The freshman class of BH-BL pose in front of the school in 1938. They are, from left to right, as follows: (first row) C. Foss, J. Collins, J. Kimball, R. Rivenburg, D. Bates (class president), J. Little, R. VanPatten, C. Vincent, M. Liebert, D. Miller, and G. White; (second row) C. Rix, M. Ryder, G. Rowledge, J. Carp, B. Steitler, B. Clough, advisors J. Gosch, L. Warren, ? Reisenger; A. Caldwell, E. Brockman, C. Ferris, D. Barnett, D. Pickney, and J. Wescott; (third row) J. McKain, S. Witbeck, L. Callahan, M. Curtis, B. VanWie, R. Cunningham, E. Feeney, C. Fisler, M. Carrigan, M. Casey, E. Constantine, H. Martini, M. Tonks, D. Burton, B. Collins, F. Kovarovic, and M. Jackson; (fourth row) G. Wetherill, R. Brockhurst, G. Lolakowski, H. Robinson, R. Johnson, F. Nittman, P. Wheeler, M. Wait, F. Resue, J. Holmes, J. Mean, M. Boswell, R. VanValkenburg, D. Smith, and E. Kolor; (fifth row) H. Abbs, W. Riddle, D. Millington, R. Lamb, R. Boyles, R. Mahar, Q. Little, W. Kinns, H. Nittman, R. Fowler, R. Weidman, J. Slover, G. Donley, M. Hatlee, and W. Niles.

My dear Edna,

I am still at the old stand doing business but not as strong, as my illness gave me quite a setback. I thought last fall and winter that I was still a fellow yet. It is hard to curb oneself when there is so much to be done. A retired life never did appeal to me.

We have been having some trouble in our school. Some of the students took the matter in hand to ask Mr. Cruickshank to resign and if he did not accede to their demands, there would be a walk-out. The Board heard about it and persuaded them for the time being not to do so. That was on Tuesday. By Friday afternoon, about 40 walked out and paraded themselves on the streets with a banner demanding justice as they thought we had not dealt fairly in punishing some and not others. All back now except five who will not return. I spent three days and nights over the affair.

Mr. Upham is the man enjoying himself when he is doped up enough to feel good. He only worries about having a good time and is booked up as who to call on next. I think it is fine that he can have his second childhood.

Last week I heard different men talk about aviation. There is a new airport between here and Schenectady. It is expected that it will do quite a business. There is a drive on to raise $100,000 by selling stock. I am not sure about this aviation thing. I don't think it will last.

I noticed today that your house is painted white. You are not the only one who has new clothes. I have a new suit, but the weather has not been warm enough for me to wear it.

I had quite a visit with Antoinette. Chance for gossip. I intend to visit with my friend, Walter Feeney tomorrow. You must remember him. He's the one that lives next door to the Hawkwood mansion.

Don't know how many misspelled words you will find.

Your friend,

F.B. Coons

The Schenectady County Airport opened in 1928 and was considered a marvel of the day. A crowd of well-wishers greeted Charles Lindbergh when he visited.

Guy Baker lived at Hawkwood, west of Middle Line Road. This house was once the home of Edward Delevan. Guy, pictured here, married Countess Louisa Irene Palma Dicisonla. They were world travelers and brought their art treasures back to Hawkwood. Guy died in 1929, "a poor and broken" man. Confederate money has been found in the windmill by this house.

Pictured in 1921, from left to right, are Walter Feeney (holding his son Donald), Mary Slade (Walter's wife), Austin and Catalina Slade (Mary's parents), and Ruth Baumgartner (Mary's sister).The man on the right in the back is unidentified. All these families lived in Ballston Center.

My dear Edna,

The good old summertime has finally arrived. There are many more cars going north than ever before. I am writing this while waiting for my folks to get ready to go somewhere—don't know where yet. We have had some nice trips. One to Greenfield to call on relatives and visit an old cemetery where my great grandfather on the Burton side is buried. I have become more interested in my ancestors. We had another flat, so there goes $15.50 for a new tube and tire.

Now, how about you? Have you been appointed to fill Miss Jones' vacancy?

I have been well fed up on aviation of late. Reading a lot about it in the newspapers and even visited the planes at the airport.

The school situation has died down. Mr. Cruickshank intends to stay. If it was me, I would quietly look for another place. The way it is here, most of the teachers are hired in the winter for the coming year. Our commencement was quite an affair this year.

I have not gotten a letter from you in a long time. Let me know if there is a problem. Must close.

FBC

Graduation from high school was a two-day event. Class Day was on Saturday. A celebration was held on the lawn of the school, and a king and queen were chosen. In this 1938 photograph, King Walter Lamb escorts Queen Lois Kinns. There was a tea dance on Saturday evening, and on Sunday, diplomas were handed out at a baccalaureate ceremony in the school's auditorium.

Frank Coons's family plot is in the Calvary Episcopal Church cemetery. Buried here are his parents, Solomon and Louisa; Frank; and his two wives, Maria and Edna.

The employees of the Ballston Lake Post Office pose. They are, from left to right, postmasters Lewis Sears and William Egan Sr. and clerks Anita Wagner and Adam Brady.

Burnt Hills, NY
September 26, 1927

My dear Edna,

This is the first opportunity I have had to answer your interesting letter. I have been away on trips and when home, there is so much work to do, specially this time of the year-filling silos, etc. Tonight I am alone with the three boys. If the little ones wake up, I am to pacify them, which I can do well as any woman. Amelia and Riley have gone down to the schoolhouse to hear Mr. Shorey give a lecture about Greece and show some pictures he took of that country. I wanted to go very much as he is an interesting speaker, but I insisted on their going as I get to hear many good speakers, see how unselfish I am. I went up to Ballston to hear a speaker talk about Italy. No wonder you are so anxious to go there.

Well, how are you? I thought you looked well and strong when you were here, did not see as your dieting had much an effect on your figure or have you cut that out to let nature have her way. I wish I could gain weight. I eat enough and still weigh 2 ounces less than a straw hat. Did not think Mary looked well at all.

Mr. Upham's community sing was a great success. Will have another next month. I was worrying as Mr. Shorey's meeting was on the same night. He was to have given his last Thursday, but it was moved ahead because of the Tunney-Dempsey fight. Mr. Robson was down to listen in as we have a new radio. If this is getting boring, don't read any more.

On your birthday, how did it feel to reach the age of discretion or near to it? I could write more, but it would require an extra stamp. I won't look this over for corrections. You can do that.
Sincerely yours,
F.B. Coons

Jack Dempsey was a good friend of Father Daniel Hogan. He poses with the boys at Father Hogan's boxing camp on Saratoga Lake in 1927. The boys, from left to right, are as follows: (front row) Joe Ross, Barry Vrooman, Stephen Kavoravic, Albert Sarto, Nick Mancini, Edward Kimball, and Michael Sarto (partially shown); (back row) Albert Quackenbush, Lester Ryder, Jack Dempsey, Father Hogan, Rudolph Sauerbrev, William Egan, Elihu Quackenbush, and Emil Kavoravic.

The Jones-Shorey house is located at 54 Lakehill Road. It was built in 1793 by Ebenezer Jones. This homestead has remained in the family for over 200 years.

Mary Ryerson Jones, a descendant of Ebenezer Jones, was the wife of George Shorey. She sits with baby Isabel on their front porch in 1912. Their other children were named George, Mary, and James. Their father was the noted artist.

Burnt Hills, NY
October 25, 1927

My dear Edna,

This will not be as long a letter as the last one as I rather outdid myself, besides I have little to write about. We have had a delightful fall. I have so enjoyed my trips to the New England coast. The houses and lawns are kept neat. They seem wiser than we in saving money and spending it carefully.

Since I last wrote to you I attended the sesquicentennial of the Battle of Saratoga on October 8th. It was a most beautiful sight with a sham battle at the close. A large number of people took part and the crowds and the automobiles one of the largest I have ever seen. We were hours getting out of a jam. So many of our ancestors from Burnt Hill fought at that important battle.

I saw your mother Sunday and inquired about Mary. She said she was better. Does she still board with the Ketchums?

I have had the other house painted as it needed it, now there are three houses on this street that look better. Your flowers in the boxes lasted until recently.

What is the matter with your football team? Union is doing fine. We have had many fine games this season at the school.

I often think of my visit to Columbus last winter, even if it did create quite a commotion. I may repeat the route this year.

I understand Miss Clarke is leaving your Mother as it is too lonesome there. She is going down to Ballston Lake with the other teachers. Most of our teachers live together on East Side Drive, although I have no idea how they keep warm in those camps.

Sincerely yours,

F.B. Coons

One of the teams which competed in the fall was the soccer team. In 1951, the members, from left to right, are as follows; (front row) R. Campbell, R. Nessle, R. Boice, T. Stern, R. Romac, and T. Kenyon; (back row) Coach W. Reid, M. DuBois, E. Chase, E. Weeks, E. Reindfleisch, D. Little, A. Digiuseppe, and Assistant Coach Rentz. The team was known as The Hillers, and Bob Boice was a leading scorer.

"Ice cream soda!
Ginger ale pop!
Burnt Hills High School
Is always on the top."

These were the junior varsity cheerleaders in 1946. The girls, from left to right, are as follows: (front row) Evelyn Dadez, Frances Nessle, Carol Parent, Beverly Bates, and Lillian Van Wie; (back row) Miss Rounds and Phillis Laws.

The marching band of BH-BL posed on the front lawn of the school in 1949.

My dear Edna,

How do you like my new stationery? I presume it is up to date. It was a birthday present from the children. It should last some time. Your boyfriend and I must be in the same class in regard to writing. You should know men are not given to writing letters as a rule.

I thought about you on Thanksgiving, being alone. You were probably invited out to your friends, but that is one day a person wants to be with their relatives.

I got all ready to attend church services this morning, but it rained very hard. One should not let a little rain deter one, but that is the way for us poor miserable sinners. I did the next best thing and heard a speaker and sacred music on the radio. You have never said if you have a radio or not. If not, get one. It will bring you hours of pleasure.

Do you come home for the holidays? It will be a long time if you wait for the vacation season. You no doubt need a lot of rest by this time. I hope you come as it gives a break for your friends and gives people something to talk about, which they are much in need of.

Well, I finally bought the rug, so "Pop" came through again. It is much nicer than the one I planned to buy, but the "Mrs." was there, so you see I am easily influenced for a tightwad. Are you for Governor Smith for President next year? Christmas will be here before we know it. Seals have been sent to me, but have not bought cards yet. Time is up so will keep the rest for next time.

Sincerely yours,

FBC

The Calvary Episcopal Church was founded in 1849. This photograph was taken c. 1940. This is the church that Edna and Frank attended.

Reverend Richard Barrett was one of many who honored Catherine Shorey on her birthday. Reverend Barrett served the Calvary congregation from 1969 until his retirement in 1992.

This picture is of the confirmation class of Calvary church in the early 1930s. They are, from left to right, as follows: (front row) Cheryl Markham, Amelia Denty, unidentified, Jean Ryder, Father Paul Williams, unidentified, Helen Roblee, Catherine Roblee, and Mildred Swatling; (back row) Fred Kingsbury, Jack Mengel, Charles Kingsbury, Etta Larkin, Arthur Mengel, Minnie Swatling, Robert Morey, Arthur Ryder, and Mattie Ashdown.

This photograph is of the interior of Calvary as it appeared in 1953.

The Lecture, or Fellowship Hall, was built in 1877. It was originally one story with horse stalls in the basement. Dancing and card games were banned, but these rules were eventually forgotten. Amateur dramatics, harvest suppers, and lectures were given here.

58

Five

1928

Mrs. Jackson and
Elizabeth

Mrs. Anna Jackson was postmistress for
Burnt Hills and organist for the
Episcopal church. Her daughter
Elizabeth was born in 1911.

My dear Edna,

This past week has been very busy with much mental, physical and social stress, but I am still going strong. I meant to write earlier in the week and mail it when I went to Rotary in Schenectady, but I could not make that meeting. I will have to make it up in Ballston next Monday. I was out four nights and had a business caller on the fifth night. I have attended two banquets. One was the third annual banquet of the Citizens Trust for the stockholders. There was good music and nicely gowned women, which would have appealed to you. The men don their best dress. FBC did the same. You have never seen me all done up, not bad for a farmer. The other affair was given locally by the firemen, about 30 attended and we had a really good time, a lively crowd, good eats, music, singing, speaking by all. I was called on as you can imagine.

Want to mention the fact that I had a very enjoyable visit the afternoon you left, I trust it was the same for you while we waited for your train. Your choice of a present shows good taste, how much better to have something useful, and I infer pretty also.

I have read part of the "President's Daughter" and don't approve of the book. I would not want children to read it am disgusted with the author.

How did you make out with the degree you were going for? You must have it by now. I have not bought my desk dictionary yet, so don't look for errors until I get one. Expect a good night's sleep as I have a busy week ahead.

Sincerely yours,

F.B. Coons

The Burnt Hills Nepture Fire Department was formed in 1918. The original firehouse was on the west side of Kingsley Road, and it was built by the department's members. The men in the photo, from left to right, are Judge Pop Wemple, Bill Gorman, Al Frieberg, and Harry Wetsel.

The membership of the Ballston Lake Fire Department in 1938 included the following, from left to right: (first row) Henry Noonan, Leroy Parsons, Lewis Ross, Bill Egan, Joe Santarchangelo, Chief Pete Sarto, Lewis Eger, Charles Markham, Carl Piercy, Harold Hackett, and Thomas McDonough; (second row) James Broderick, Charles Manzer, Herb Ketchum, Harry Mead, Earl Clogston, James Sullivan, Clarence Hansen, John Sarto, Frances Lameroux, Edward Sutphen, and Clarence Burrus; (third row) Larry ?, Robert Kimball, Cedric Gillingham, Donald Sutphen, Nicholas Mancini, Michael Sarto, and Everett Nessell. Note the sign over the door. It seems that the word "Lake" was an afterthought.

This 1929 photograph, taken by the noted photographer Howard Humes, depicts the Eagle-Matt Lee Fire Department on Bath Street. The fire company was formed in 1816 and is the second oldest in continuance in New York state. The *Ballston Journal* building is on the left, and the railroad station is on the right.

Burnt Hills, NY
February 21, 1928

My dear Edna,

It is rather late to start writing. May have to finish tomorrow. My namesake has just gone to his room and Dorothy has gone to a mother-daughter banquet with Mrs. Cruickshank — they expect about 300 to attend. So I am all alone for once, free of any confusion.

For six weeks, a physician from Schenectady has been coming here every day to take care of the sick. It started with one of the little fellows and he has had constant care until now. Then all of the family required attention. Riley was real bad and when the doctor got here on Friday, he said he must go to the hospital. So, the ambulance came and took him, just nine years ago this month his mother was taken from the house. He is slowly improving. He has to have absolute quiet and no one is allowed in. He asked for me, so I saw him for a few minutes. You are probably asking what is the cause of this. I understand it is a new germ or bug recently discovered. With Riley they injected a powerful serum in the veins. We could call it a case of quinsy, but they don't.

How is the political situation? Are you for Senator Willis or Hoover? Also, between Hoover and Smith. Although Smith is a democrat, he is also an Irish Catholic. I don't believe I ever heard you express what party you adhere to.

This is the time of year we hire teachers. Most of them will stay. There are some in the community who don't care for Mr. Cruickshank so we thought it best to let him go for the good of the school. What is unfortunate this time is that Lieut. Bailey is away for some time and he is the only scholarly one and the one most competent to choose a new principal.

I could finish this much easier by talking to you.

Sincerely yours,

FBC

Ellis Hospital is named for John Ellis, the founder of Alco. The hospital opened its doors on Nott Street in 1906.

The Ballston Lake Rescue Squad's first ambulance was a 1936 used LaSalle hearse. In 1951, the squad's first year in existence, they answered two calls. In 1997, they responded to 700 calls.

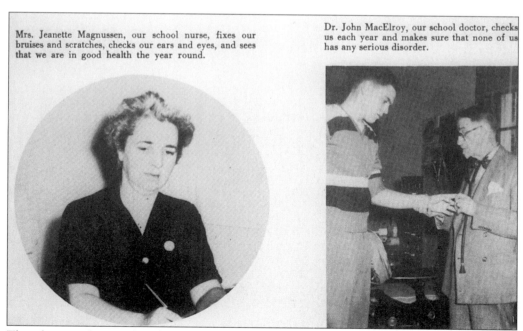

Mrs. Jeanette Magnussen, our school nurse, fixes our bruises and scratches, checks our ears and eyes, and sees that we are in good health the year round.

Dr. John MacElroy, our school doctor, checks us each year and makes sure that none of us has any serious disorder.

This photograph was taken from the 1954 BH-BL yearbook.

Burnt Hills, NY
March 18, 1928

My dear Edna,

Your last letter was interesting as usual and perhaps I am reading into it, especially the part relating to your illness. Cheer up. It must be hard to be away from your family when you are ill. It is too bad that you don't like your doctor. We have trusted old Doc Cotton for years.

Have you moved into that new apartment yet or do you have to take a course in home making first? You say you are strong with salads and faulty at pies. One is never too old to learn. Start with apple and report how you succeeded. You will enjoy your apartment where you can entertain your friends—lady friends that is.

Believe me, I have spent some time on school affairs and some worry as to who to choose for a new principal. I have been swamped with applications, as they say, the woods are full of them. Most of the candidates send their picture and the ladies send their age, height, weight, personality characteristics, size and experience. No small ones or over large if I had my way. The one I have chosen is 130 pounds, 5 feet 7 inches tall.

Tuesday night I go to Ballston to attend the annual beefsteak dinner of the Utopian Society. I have been a member for nearly 20 years. I will wear my good suit. When you are out with money people you have to throw a bluff and let them think you are one of them.

As I have exceeded the usual allotment of paper, I will close.

Sincerely yours,

F.B. Coons

Author's note—The Riverwood Inn was a dinner and dance hall outside of Scotia. It featured jazz music, which was a new form of music in the 1920s, and exemplified another revolt from the convention.

Dr. John Cotton established his practice in Burnt Hills around 1878. An office was set up at his house, and a visit to the doctor cost 50¢. He delivered babies, set bones, and pulled teeth. This photograph was taken in front of his house in 1938, when he was 88 years old.

Edward and Maude Moore were "money people" and they lived in the Buell Mansion during the twenties. The carriage stone in the front yard has "S.W. Buell" etched into it.

The living room was furnished with the finest. "The Buell" was one of the first houses to have gas lights.

My dear Edna,

Did you get the announcement of the marriage of Gilbert and Betty? I did and were so much surprised that the event had taken place. The next matter to arouse the curious minded is what Antoinette is going to do—marry Ashley or not. She could do much worse as he is a fine fellow. We often go on the bus together. I had a long visit with her a short time ago and she said she was going to Europe. She can take care of herself all right as she is a bright woman. She has the money too. Gilbert never would call his father-in-law Father Bogart before. I think he has been Rector here for six years. What will he do now? I noticed they are having water run to the house and presume a bathroom.

You spoke of the strain on the pocketbook. It did give me quite a jolt that I was part of the expense. A little bad luck can happen now and then and someone has to pay the bills. It may hurt some but it is a good lesson to learn. Enough said. Just change your mind about me being a tightwad. I admit that I am to a certain extent and proud of it.

Riley has not fully recovered. I think he had a nervous breakdown with his illness. He does not care to work, in fact, he has sold out his business interest in the grocery store to the Bailey's. Before the "Bishop" died it was old Nate, young Nate and young Nate's son. Now it is only Nathan.

I was invited to the Lecture Hall the other night to meet Rev. Mr. Boise, who I expect will be the new clergyman. He is a good worker and will build up the congregation if any one can.

Sincerely yours,

FBC

Ashley Baker's parents were Colonel Benjamin Baker and Harriett Bayeux. They married in 1857. Their other children were Guy, William, Mary, Benjamin, George, and Edith. Benjamin Baker Sr. was a graduate of Yale and served in the Civil War. When the slain President Lincoln's body was carried through Albany, Colonel Baker was a member of the Honor Guard. The couple spent their last years in Burnt Hills.

Benjamen Baker lived at 172 Kingsley Road. Doctor Augustus Sitterly lived next door.

William Bliss Baker built his home and artist studio, known as "the Castle," on East Side Drive. His paintings are preserved at the Smithsonian. He died in 1886, at the age of 26. Gus Smith later owned the property and rented rooms.

My dear Edna,

If I had command of our language as you have I could write a nice long letter, but I am not as gifted.

Did not see Mary when she was here. I am told she has a new car. If so, you will want to ride around this summer with her and will not are to go with me. I so look forward to our annual one day trip, please don't disappoint. My old car rides easy and runs fine. Why get rid of something just because it is old? I wish I could have retained my youthful good looks and kept back the fleeting years as well as you have, not saying you are in my class though. If I were like Mr. Upham, I would be seeking the young flappers to go around with and get all the pleasures of the modern life. Speaking of Mr. Upham, he visits us often and runs on and on, most of it we have heard before.

You know I have not seen Gilbert or Betty since they were married. I seldom go up to get the mail, so I may make a special trip to call on them. They were not serenaded much to my surprise, although it was so intended as we were invited by Nathan to be there on a certain night. I went up to wait, but no one showed up, so we played cards.

I don't think lady luck has forsaken me with the bull stock market that has been going on for some time. Maybe I should get out of the game, I have had some handsome profits.

The North Road has been closed some time for repairs, so we get all the traffic. Seems like old times again.

Your letters are appreciated and I give them more than a once over.

Sincerely yours,

F.B. Coons

The compulsion to buy an automobile in the 1920s seemed to effect all classes, rich and poor alike, irrespective of need or personal budget. Owning an automobile was the ultimate status symbol. Many villagers in Burnt Hills claimed to be the first to own a car. This 1915 Ford touring car had no side windows. Curtains were used during inclement weather.

Flappers were independent-minded young women of the 1920s. The term is derived from a young bird "flapping" its wings in an attempt to fly. Flappers were known to be bold and unconventional in dress and behavior. Flappers would have enjoyed the fun and excitement of White's Beach, an amusement park on the west banks of Ballston Lake. It was opened in 1932. Old-timers recall working to dig out the mud to make the swimming area.

SECTION OF PICNIC GROUNDS AT THE
WHITE BEACH ON BEAUTIFUL SPRING-FE[
BALLSTON LAKE, N.Y.

Many school and church picnics were held at White's Beach. A boat-shaped diner provided hamburgers and hot dogs for the beach-goers. White's Beach was located near the settlement of the first white men in Ballston, i.e. the McDonald brothers, who came in 1763.

Burnt Hills, NY
July 1, 1928

My dear Edna,

Your last letter carried so much weight that it was held at the post office until I came up with two cents, don't mind the cost when one gets such an interesting letter. Also, perhaps someone's curiosity at the post office will be aroused. It was not clear in my mind when it was you leaving on your vacation. I would like to make an appointment to meet you in Albany as you suggested.

Saw Mary down at the school exercises. I have tried several times to call on her, but have failed. She may as well be satisfied if I don't, although I cannot make myself believe that this is true, even if she did not want to go to Riverwood Inn last winter. We are all entitled to some pleasure in this world. I have not been to the Riverwood, but expect to invite some friends soon as I do not entertain at home.

Our school exercises went off smoothly. The Commencement was for the largest and best class yet and the auditorium was filled. I sat on the stage, which should be considered an honor. We also had a class day this year. The community has reason to be proud of the school, at least I am. I agree with you that we should do more in restriction of the young drivers. There is no reason why they cannot ride the bicycles until they are eighteen. There have been two accidents this spring. One of our students drove off the bridge at the Outlet. Fortunately, no one drowned.

I would like to go down to Ashbury Park. That is a trip you would like since you care so much for the ocean.

Yours,

F.B.C.

The bridge over the outlet of Ballston Lake was once made of wooden planks. An article written in 1827 in the *Philadelphia Album* states, "In the township of Ballston, there is a spot, upon which nature has lavished her gifts with an unsparing hand. At the bottom of a valley, there is a sheet of water known as Long Lake. To avoid a circuit of several miles, a single canoe—the hollowed trunk of a pine—has been constructed by the country people for the benefit of those who wish to visit the opposite shore. About midway on the northern bank, there are the remains of an artificial landing and an old house." The article continues to relate that the house was once owned by a Tory who was hanged for treason during the Revolution and that his ghost appeared to locals after he was buried in the village graveyard.

School bus drivers often know more about the students than other school employees. In 1951, the drivers, from left to right, were Mr. Heckman, Mr. Morgan, Mr. Englehart, Mr. Dussault, Mr. Merchant, and Mr. Wetsel.

Ben Heckman drove one of BH-BL's early school buses. This one was painted maroon and white and could seat 40 people. He recalled that the students were well behaved, and the boys dressed in suits and ties.

Burnt Hills, NY
September 18, 1928

My dear Edna,

Your letter received with a heartfelt welcome. I take it you have been busy catching up on all the work you missed when you left so hurriedly for home, but then work is a great panacea for one who has had a great sorrow come into their life. It diverts the thoughts and helps rid oneself of the lonesome feeling.

By the way, I got my $1.50 back from the Hotel Johnston along with an apology for the over-charge. This is the 15th anniversary of Riley and Amelia's wedding. They have taken the Robsons over to Riverwood Inn to celebrate. What did you do to celebrate the event of September 12th? You know it is a long time to live. Did you have more roses sent to you? I am curious to know who sent the ones you wrote about.

I found a letter the other day in my coat pocket that Mary wrote, thanking me for the recommendation and the ride to Manchester. Perhaps you remember that trip. I shall keep the letter in memory of her and keep it with all of your letters. Perhaps some day I can get them printed in a book.

There was an interesting article in the newspaper about schools and old fashioned discipline. The man who wrote it was 92 years old and attended one of our rural school houses. It seems that the teacher used a switch on the students. I am glad that those days are over.

I often think of the very pleasant times we had together when you were home, even if we had to go away to find meeting places — Saratoga, Proctor's, The Van Curler and the last, but not the least, the Edison Club. All the rides and dinners for the whole month of August. I am sorry if you feel we were too discreet in our behavior, but under the circumstances, what else could we do? The days of the old fashioned parlor are gone, and the auto has taken its place. Better not say any more as I might digress from being formal.

Sincerely yours,

F.B. Coons

Author's note — September 12th was Edna's birthday.

W. Chinski, R. Dawley, B. Grams, D. Hyde, E. Keefe, K. Plummer, G. Rogers, H. Stewart, E. Thibodeau.
L. Vincent, R. Wagner, G. West, M. Wiley, R. Schilling, J. Nicholls, D. Scheibel, C. Allen, M.
Armstrong, M. Bublak, I. Esposito, M. Fetter, J. Hoyle, L. Kimball, C. Leavitt, K. Maxwell, S. Miller,
R. Sluti, T. Szat, A. Voekringer, C. Bailey, F. Billington, S. Chambers, P. Cichy, J. Cunningham, N.
Davis, J. Duguette, D. Graves, N. Jacobson, F. Kovorovic, R. McIntyre, J. Price, G. Reckner, D.
Shorey, M. Slovacek, J. Sommerman, D. Wait, P. Hartman, D. Kuty, P. Mitchell, R. Paquin, M. Sarto.
J. Strylet, P. Thibodeau, M. Wallbillig, J. Welldon, J. Van Dorn, Mrs. Youmans, Mrs. Reid.

P. M. FIRST &

PRE FIRST

These two pictures were taken from the 1947 yearbook entitled *The Hilltop*. These children were "spared the rod."

W. Adam, G. Brown, K. Cleveland, T. Cooke, R. Fiske, J. Frates, D. Getty, L. Laird, D. Lambert,
D. Lyall, L. Maranville, W. Melanson, D. Miller, D. Parker, F. Waldbillig, R. Wetsel, J. Wheeler, D. Zeh.
I. Allen, J. Brewster, N. Coons, N. Curtis, E. Freitag, G. Garrison, S. Guest, E. Jensen, J. Kenyon.
J. Marks, G. Olin, M. Parskocim, E. Resue, P. Stevens, B. Wahn, J. Bradley, Miss Rice.

SIXTH GRADE

73

Burnt Hills, NY
November 11, 1928

My dear Edna,

When one has something to look forward to, the time seems to go by slowly. So, next week you should be home in front of your own fireside enjoying the company of your friends and relatives.

We were away for three days down to the Catskills and New Jersey. The first part of the trip was the one I had planned to take you and Mary on if she had lived.

We had a supper at the Calvary Hall Saturday night. It was to raise money to enclose the small porch on the Rectory for the daughter, Mary, who is ill with TB. This week the Rotary is to have a tour of the General Electric Company. That will take the whole afternoon. That night, we have a school meeting. We have the largest enrollment this year. I fear we will outgrow the school.

As for the political scene, I understand Antoinette believes that anyone who is a Democrat must be lacking in good sense. Are you still of the same opinion that you will vote for Smith. I doubt if I will as I do not approve of his attitude of the prohibition question. Think he has said more about it than is called for. Neither do I warm up to Hoover. If I vote for him, it will be the first time I have voted for a Republican. I am glad Roosevelt got elected. I think he will make a good Governor. How much have you cleaned up on this Hoover bull market? I have sold one stock, but am hanging onto the others.

Been doing a little papering. My two rooms have been done. I have to repair the roof on the ice house as soon as I can.

I have but a short time before listening to President Coolidge in honor of this day. This evening I intend to call on the Stewarts as Mr. E.A. Stewart died yesterday.

You will have to keep the picture as I have not had another taken. Not much on getting my picture done. I am glad you have recovered from you illness. Don't worry about losing weight. We figured it out that the more you weigh, the less you are worth per pound.

Betty has a new fur coat. Gilbert bought it for her in Canada. She told me it was their wedding trip. I don't feel beneath her although I am of the common herd.

If you have an extra photo send it along as I could use it.

Your loyal friend,

F.B. Coons

Prohibition (1920–1933) was a time of homemade bathtub gin, rum-running, speakeasies, and bootlegging. The later term comes from the practice of carrying illegal spirits in the tops of boots. One local speakeasy was Kristels. It was raided and closed in 1931. A large gristmill was on the property, and it was torn down in 1928. Homemade brew was stored in the sheds by the mill.

The school did grow, and by 1954, there were plans of building a new high school and a need for a traffic squad to control noise and traffic flow in the halls. The senior squad, from left to right, are as follows: (front row) M. Cunningham, M. Phillips, and M. Stahl; (second row) M. Knapp, L. Voelker, and J. Stewart; (third row) P. Bates, D. Campbell, and B. Barbera; (fourth row) J. Carpenter, R. Hartman, and M. McIntyre; (fifth row) T. Bates, C. Lundy, and G. Isley.

Until the invention of electric refrigerators, icehouses were a necessity. Ice was stored in sawdust, and it could last up to a year. Ice was harvested from Ballston Lake and hauled by teams of horses. Many a tale is told of losing teams of horses when they broke through the ice.

Edward Sutphen portrays ice harvesting on Ballston Lake for commercial purposes. Ice was transported by the railroad to nearby cities.

Six
1929

Adam Gartner

Adam Gartner was born in Burnt Hills in 1914, the son of John and Rosetta Gartner. The Jacob Gartner farm was on the corner of Jacob Street and Lakehill Road.

Burnt Hills, NY
January 17, 1929

My dear friend Edna,

I have been sick in bed for a week. I will recover fully soon and get back my usual vigor. I meant to go to Schenectady today, but did not because of the storm. The sickness has gone through the whole house. Our good maid is still going strong.

I just took a break from writing to hear Franklin D. Roosevelt over the radio. He is some speaker. Try to hear him.

I am to have dinner with E.S. Coons, my lawyer and spend the afternoon with him. That will mean another trip to Ballston Spa. I hope the roads are in good shape as I intent to take the back way past your old neighborhood.

On January 28th there will be the annual stockholders dinner of the Citizen Trust Company and it will be held at the Van Curler. The mid-winter supper is to be held at the church, and the men are in charge. We have planned roast pork and mashed potatoes. The newspaper said it was an event, "at which time the men endeavor to show the women that it takes masculine intelligence to do such things right." I wonder what kind of response that will bring. I also plan on taking my people to Proctor's as a special treat.

I will bid you good-by for now.

Your friend,

F.B. Coons

Proctor's Theater was opened in 1925. It was a 3,000-seat showplace with marble staircases and a Wurlizer organ.

Edna Davis's old neighborhood included the Alvah Larkin farm. It is located at the corner of Charlton Road and Goode Street.

A plow was used to pull the trolley through the snow on Front Street in Ballston Spa. E.S. Coons was a lawyer who had his office at 58 Front Street.

My dear Edna,

As you can see I have changed my writing paper. I want to congratulate you on getting the solitaire game. I seldom can do it. I have got my ice in, so am free to make the trip most any time now. I had thoughts of leaving here on the 21st, arriving in Columbus the next morning and from there to Washington.

Mr. Boys has started a men's community club which will meet monthly. About 25 attended. We started with a song service, his talk on Japan, then refreshments and then cards. School was closed today due to the snow storm. That is a rare occurrence here as we are hardy souls. Personally, I will be glad to get away for a bit.

It will be ten years tomorrow that I was left alone. That was a blow worse than death, but time has been the great healer of sorrow.

Your sincere friend,

F.B. Coons

Schoolchildren enjoyed an occasional "school is closed due to snow" day. Dr. Cotton's house is shown in the background.

No matter how cold it was outside, students at BH-BL were assured a hot noon-time meal. Catherine Kinns (pictured on the right) served as cafeteria manager from 1932 until 1963. In the early years, she made the meals herself, multiplying her home recipes. She is remembered as making the very best macaroni and cheese. In those days ketchup was not considered a vegetable! This photograph was taken from the 1946 yearbook.

The cafeteria was in the basement of the school, as seen in this 1954 photograph.

My dear Edna,

Our letters must have passed each other. No harm done. I have not changed my plans. Last night I invited Riley to go with me to Ballston to attend the annual beefsteak supper at the Utopia Club. We brought some home for Amelia. They send for the beef from Boston and then the men cook it. You know there are some things that men do better than women.

My train will get in early in the morning, so do not get up to meet me, unless you want to. If you are not there I will go to the Fort Hayes Hotel.

Went to Ballston the other day and did something much to your advantage. Have I aroused your curiosity? Perhaps you can get me to say when I see you as I don't have many secrets that you do not know about. I have not seen your mother, but will try to see her before I leave. I will not tell her where I am going as it might stir up gossip.

I have no new clothes for my trip, so don't parade me around.

I remain, your friend,

F.B. Coons

[Author's note-according to Frank's bank ledger, he withdrew $300 and marked "ring" on this date.]

The soldiers monument in Ballston Spa was erected in 1888. It is in honor of veterans of the Revolutionary War, the War of 1812, and the Mexican and Civil Wars.

One of the attractions of going to Ballston Spa was to get one's picture taken by Jesse Wooley. He is pictured here in an early internal combustion vehicle.

Another Ballston Spa attraction was the Saratoga County Fair, first held in 1841. The current site, on Fair Ground Avenue, was purchased in 1899.

My dear Pal,

In addressing you this way, it reminds me of a song "that wonderful pal of mine." You were so disappointed that you could not experience the thrill we had been talking about, so much on account of it being a public place when we parted at the station.

I was expecting to go to Mount Vernon this morning, but the bus did not go on account of rain. I have met your cousin, Mr. Ketchum and got in his good graces. It is apparent that they have not been informed about our friendship. Just as well to leave them in the dark.

I may visit the Smithsonian tomorrow. They have an exhibit on farm life in the United States. It would probably be easier to remain in the hotel, read a bit and recall the exhibits we have at Ballston during the annual summer fair. At least it was warm on those occasions. Hoover is to be inaugurated here in a few days, so the city is very busy. I wonder if the celebrations will be as heartfelt as the ones we have at home. He seems to be all right, even though he is a Republican and a Quaker. Worse things could happen.

I had a lovely lady to entertain me in Columbus. Lieut. Bailey would have said, "charming." Would have enjoyed staying there longer. Thank you for the good time.

Sincerely,

F.B. Coons

There is nothing as heartwarming as a home-town parade. Shirley Merchant is the baton twirler for the BH-BL band as it marched north on Kingsley Road in 1950. Walter Beck marched with his band. He is the man with the white hair, wearing the white suit.

On special occasions, Forest Park had fireworks. It was advertised as a "Brilliant illumination of park and lake. Grand finale—Naval Bombardment."

TWILIGHT SPECIAL
FOR
FOREST PARK

TIME TABLE EFFECTIVE JUNE 24, 1910

	WEEK DAYS	SUNDAYS
MOHAWK AVENUE, SCOTIA	7:45 P.M.	7:15 P.M.
WAITING ROOM	8:00 P.M.	7:30 P.M.
STATE AND McCLELLAN STS.	8:08 P.M.	7:38 P.M.
UNION AND McCLELLAN STS.	8:12 P.M.	7:42 P.M.
WENDELL AVE. AND RUGBY ROAD	8:15 P.M.	7:45 P.M.
HATTIE ST. AND VAN VRANKEN AVE.	8:20 P.M.	7:50 P.M.
ALPLAUS	8:33 P.M.	8:03 P.M.
FOREST PARK	8:45 P.M.	8:15 P.M.

THIS CAR WILL LEAVE MOHAWK AVENUE, SCOTIA, EVERY FAIR EVENING AND WILL RUN VIA STATE STREET, McCLELLAN STREET, RUGBY ROAD AND WENDELL AVENUE TO FOREST PARK, BALLSTON LAKE

DANCING EVERY WEEK-DAY AFTERNOON & EVENING

SUNDAY CONCERTS AFTERNOON AND EVENING

RUBENS ORCHESTRA

ARRANGE TO SPEND THE HOT SUMMER EVENINGS AT FOREST PARK, IT IS ALWAYS COOL AND REFRESHING

The Odd Fellows Hall was decorated in 1915 to celebrate 50 years after the end of the Civil War. Under the bust of Abraham Lincoln, was a sign, "With malice toward none, with charity for all."

My dear Edna,

I see you don't date your letters any more. Is that the proper way to do it now? I have to depend on you to inform me of such matters as I live in the country.

Easter was a fine day. I assume you attended services. I did not have anything new to wear and did notice not many had. Dorothy had a new coat and hat and looked very pretty. I see you have had two dinner parties. That must be tiresome for one on a diet and who is not use to cooking.

I have been very busy with school affairs. We had school in session in one week, largely due to the efforts of Mr. Smith, located in five different places partitions put in, seats borrowed from Ballston and Scotia, blackboards on the walls. Seems like old times. We are growing in numbers, 12 new pupils therefore a larger building is planned for the future. It will be some time before we can erect a new building due to red tape. An architect has been engaged, same one we employed for the other building. Amount of insurance totaled $75,000. Hope they will allow the full amount. May 5th is the vote on the proposition to erect a new building and remodel the present one. The cost would not exceed $205,000. The State will pay 25% of the cost.

Walter Feeney is buried this afternoon. I am going to the funeral. We went to school together.

Your boyfriend,

F.B. Coons

The school burned on March 30, 1929, a Sunday morning. The cause has never been determined. A newspaper account reads, "Mr. Frank Coons called a special board of education meeting to find temporary quarters for the school." There were 333 students attending grades 1 through 12. Hundreds of people came to see the ruins of the school.

Mr. and Mrs. Elmer Pepper lived next to the school. They were awakened by the noise of the fire and spread the alarm. Six fire companies responded. Mr. Pepper was a pharmacist. His daughters, Gladys and Althea, graduated a year before the fire.

Walter Feeney posed with his sister Adda, who is standing. His wife, Mary, is seated with their children, Eleanor, Margaret, and Donald. Walter Feeney died due to complications resulting from a tooth extraction.

My dear Edna,

I found everything all right when I got home, farm work all taken care of. Now I am looking forward to a trip to Ashbury Park in August. Amelia thinks I should have gone to Europe with my friend, but that kind of trip takes money. Besides I am a farmer and harvest time is almost here. Dr. Betts and family have just left for Alaska, don't know if they will meet Orville Curtis. I like to travel, am not content to lead the quiet life.

How is the hat? Did it survive the shock and weight? I presume so, as they are long-lifed. Next time you must watch your step.

I hope the warm weather will continue as it is good for our milk business. It was a wise move to go to Schoharie County for milk. I don't suppose this is interesting to you. Sorry you are having such a lonesome time, don't wonder being all by yourself. You are a mature lady and very intelligent, so do not regret acting silly in my presence.

Our commencement exercises went well. I had the pleasure of handing out the diplomas. There were 14 this year. You will be pleased to know your nephew got one. Dorothy was chosen among the freshmen to address the seniors. She did very nicely and is growing up to be a fine looking lady. I have a new chauffeur now. Amelia has a permit and takes me wherever I want to go. She thinks it is nice of me to let her take the car, so I make some people happy.

This August I may take you to Howe's Caverns. It has just opened up. They have an elevator that takes you down 150 feet, and the caves are lit with electricity. Another sight is the electric fountain at Central Park in Schenectady. We will have some fine trips. The city folks have begun coming to the Lake for the summer season. Papa is used up. Good-night.

FBC

Ballston Lake, although beautiful, drops off to dangerous depths and is lined with shale, underwater shelves. "Cribs" were wooden structures held afloat by barrels. People could take a dip without fear of drowning. Pictured here are Audrey Philbrook and George Herman at 110 Westside Drive.

Forest Park was also known as Demerest Park. In this 1905 photograph, members of the Ballston Spa Methodist Church pose at a church picnic. Joseph Leonard Weed is the man standing next to the tree on the first balcony. He was 71 years old. Look closely—there is a brave soul on the highest balcony around the tree.

Forest Park was on the southwest portion of Ballston Lake. The trolley brought city folk to the park. This photograph by J. Wooley portrays a mother admonishing her children. Others wait in line for a ride on the *Camanche*, a steam engine-powered boat.

My dear Edna,

Just a few lines before I leave for Schenectady to let you know I will meet your train when you come from Syracuse. I hope to have the haying done by the time you come. I have been doing the hay stacks and am grateful that I can do the work.

I called on your mother and aunt Sunday night. The Ketchums are not coming because of the heat. Your mother is not well due to the effects of it. Your neighbor, Mrs. VanVetchton, is to be buried today.

Hope we can plan some nice trips while you are home. I so look forward to your annual vacation home in August. Let me know which train you will be taking, and I will meet you at the station. I hope no one sees me there.

Hoping to see you soon,

F.B. Coons

Railroad engines were made at the American Locomotive Company, which was located on the corner of Maxon Road and Nott Street. George Jordon (third from left) was one Ballstonian who worked at ALCO. The engine was made in the 1920s.

The Delaware and Hudson train derailed on July 31, 1910. The northbound trolley is pictured in this Wooley photograph. Irish immigrants lived in the village of Ballston Lake and worked on the railroad.

Georgiana and Derrak VanVechton lived at this house during the 1920s. At that time it was the next house east of the Davis house on Lakehill Road.

My dear Edna,

I have had quite a respite from writing. I much prefer to talk to you as I did for a whole month. If I remember correctly, it was decided that I did 60 percent of the talking when it should have been the other way around. I discovered that the Ketchums were here, and I intended to call on them on my way home from the barber shop, but since it was so late when I left, I did not stop.

I have decided that August is the best month. I don't think Burnt Hills is as lonesome to you as it was a few years ago. Four weeks tomorrow since you and the Coons family had that delightful ride to Speculator. It is a warm, autumnal day here. I suppose the folks will be closing their camps on the Lake soon.

A birthday comes around once a year. I believe you had one the other day. Let's see, how many does that make?

The silo is full, earlier than usual. I cut all the corn with the harvester. I presume you are back to your diet now after living so high on the hog when you were home. How about that 150 mark?

Our school is some larger this year. We have 15 teachers, not bad for the country.

We have a new radio here on trial — good tone but high in price, about $150.00. Amelia backed out about using her flower money. We will have to come up with another source if we decide to buy it.

I still don't have a photo of you, not shamed to have one taken are you? I had mine taken for Rotary last summer. I am still in the dark about the change of hearts. Have heard no gossip or rumors. Perhaps we are too old to be talked about.

Sincerely yours,

F.B. Coons

This Ballston Lake camp was located at 110 Westside Drive. Jessie and Audrey Philbrook are seated, while Mary Cecelia Campbell stands. The camp was built about 1900.

John Ellis Campbell is the young boy in the center of this picture, taken at the cottage at 108 Westside Drive.

A Union College banner hangs on the front porch of this camp, called the Outside Inn. George Yager is seated on the steps with the ball. The picture was taken in 1920. Many of the camps were summer rentals, and few people lived year-round on the lake.

My dear girl friend,

Evidently you had not received my last letter when you sent your last one or you would have had your mind eased from all worry. I could not see where you committed any error that you should be troubled about in the least. I certainly took no offense, so address you letters just as you feel.

I have been more of a gentleman farmer of late, so the time goes more slowly. Also, the holidays will not be as bright as they have been. That reminds me, when are you going to take your vacation? I am anxious to know.

I have just sent out a letter to parties looking for land for the site of a golf course. They are looking for 200 acres. It will encompass the Seelye property also on this side of the road. The Seelye house would make a fine club house without too many alterations. I saw Gilbert this week, and they are ready to sell either in part of whole. Antoinette is tired of keeping it going. These people will not do anything until spring, so it will be up in the air. Keep this to yourself. It would be nice to get some activity around here. Our streets are all too quiet most of the time, even when the weather and roads are good.

It has been icy all week, great damage up past Ballston, wires down, trees broken, no lights or power, the worst ever. It reminds me of the time you were home and needed an escort to keep you on your feet on the ice.

Be sure and get your usual present from me and complete the set. Send the bill and I will forward the money. You have my card with greetings. Don't think I was owing you this letter, so send two now.

Ever yours,

F.B. Coons

The streets of the villages of Burnt Hills and Ballston Lake were peaceful. This view is on Kingsley Road, facing north.

A man strolls down the sidewalk on Kingsley Road while a horse-drawn carriage is headed south out of the village.

This was the "fork in the bend of the road." Blue Barns Road is to the left and Kingsbury to the right. The Lansing home was in the middle.

One would see a hitching post on the left and a streetlight on the right as they approached the hill leading to "the Branch," an early name for the village of Ballston Lake.

Looking up Lakehill, one can see the Henry Schermerhorn house on the south side of the road near the top of the hill. Henry's son William was killed in World War II. The blue star on the flag, in the window of this house, was then turned to a gold star.

Seven

1930

Mrs. Sarah Stickles lived across the street
from the Methodist church. She was
born in 1833 and known to model fancy
hats and furs.

Burnt Hills, NY
May 30, 1930

My dear Pal,

I am getting better. It irks me that I went all winter without a cold and get one this time of year. No smoke, not much reading and no appetite. Been reading Mrs. Vanamee's book. It is considered a high class of literature. I will send you one. They cost $3.00. She wrote, "When Parker and I stepped off the trolley at the Burnt Hills road stop, there was nothing to be seen but the tiny box of a waiting room, and the snowy fields undulating in all directions. Presently a sleigh bell tinkled and a horse and a cutter came into view, and as it drew nearer we saw a small form cheerfully flapping the reins. Mr. Quivey told us bits of news and pointed out the sights. Soon we were slipping between Mr. Bailey's young orchards, and then we stopped at the Bailey's house at the edge of the village and were warmly welcomed before a blazing log fire. We passed the red brick Baptist Church, the old store at the corner, the quaint old hotel, then around the corner past the Seelyes' farm, then the church land—the little empty rectory on the left, and the wooden church to match across the way, then tiny sexton's cottage, and the big barn of a parish hall." Things don't change that much here.

We built a bedroom and two closets over my room to make more room for the boys. Be glad when it is done. There is too much confusion.

Sincerely,

FBC

Reverend Parker VanAmee served the Calvary Episcopal congregation from 1911 until 1916. He joined the army in World War I as a combat officer rather than a chaplain. He was killed in France in 1918. His wife, Mary, wrote his biography, entitled *Vanamee*.

Commander Claude and his wife, Emily Moore Bailey, lived at Focastle Farm. She wrote, "a sandy road ran in front of our lawn, where the ring of horse's feet and the soft roll of wheels swelled the drowsy silence of summer, and the clear music of sleigh bells delighted us during the months of deep snow."

Mr. and Mrs. Bailey pose at their retirement home at 82 Lakehill Road, known as "Three Acres." He wrote of a Memorial Day parade that passed his home, "The school band passes, flags fly, veterans endeavor to keep step, local dignitaries and a guest speaker march proudly by. Children on the sidewalks are thrilled. I hang out the flag on my front porch."

My dear Edna,

I am sorry that my letters are so short, but my ambition of late has not been very much. I have had a set back. It started with a cold and winded up with a weak pump and low blood pressure. So I am sitting around enjoying the good old summer time.

I will wait to go to Ashbury Park, may wait until August, as I may have some company by then. If I feel better and the weather permits, I may take my name-sake to Forest Park for a ride and some ice cream. Hope to write again in a week.

Sincerely,

F.B. Coons

The Forest Park dining hall is pictured in this early spring 1916 postcard. The hall and adjacent hotel seem to be waiting for the summer crowds.

This view of Forest Park was taken from the east bank of Ballston Lake. Ballston Lake was called Long Lake by the first settlers.

The Forest Park Hotel was just north of the pavilions. It was a popular place for honeymooners.

Burnt Hills, NY
June 18, 1930

My dear Edna,

I am better now, gaining weight, smoking and riding around. I sit on the porch and visit with those who walk by, mostly about school matters. I went up to see your mother, but she had gone to Seelye's and they said she had gone to your brother's and did not look well at all. Mr. Upham said she had gone because she was ill.

Believe that I had mentioned to you about the new eating place at Townley's across the street and down from here. It opened May 30th and they are having wonderful success. First class in every respect, catering to the best of people. The name is Hollyhock Inn. I was there last Monday with the other members of the school board. Will take Dorothy there soon.

The bids for the new school were opened Monday. There was a big difference between the high and low bids, some $30,000. We will use the entire $205,000 and then barely enough. The commencement exercises will be held at the Baptist Church this year.

Sincerely,

F.B. Coons

Jessie and Earl Townley posed in this 1960 photograph. They lived at 66 Lakehill Road, and Jessie ran a restaurant named the Hollyhock Inn. It was advertised as having a private dining room, which catered to bridge card parties.

The Townleys were participants in the Methodist church's annual Lords Acre auction. In 1950, the cooks for the event, from left to right, were Margaret Ward, Bill Demerest, Iona Cunningham, Luella Knight, Malida Smith, Ray Falconer, Mabel Rogers, Sue Michael, Hazel Rowledge, Jesse Townley, Nora Smith, Joe Heckler, and Ethel Demerest.

Because of the school fire, the Class of 1930 was graduated at the Burnt Hills Baptist Church. This house of worship was built in 1839.

Burnt Hills, NY
July 13, 1930

My dear Edna,

I presume you are counting the days until your annual rest period. It is a quiet time during your busy year. Your mother and other friends look forward to seeing you. I have called on your mother and Eunice Davis. I find that your mother is gaining some and in good spirits. It was nice that Miss Davis could be with her to cheer her up. She is leaving, but your Aunt Mary is coming.

My term on the school board expires August 5th, unless I am reelected to serve. The duties help break up the monotony. The building that was left we are having it put in shape and expect to have it ready when school opens in September. We may have to put in temporary stairs.

Last week, we were invited to attend a meeting of the Betts clan at the old homestead by Frank Betts. Orville and Susie were there. I expect to entertain Dr. Betts and his wife at the Hollyhock Inn this week.

Let me know your plans. I will try to meet you.

Sincerely,

F.B. Coons

Frank Betts married Adele Wheeler in 1899. She was the daughter of John Wheeler and Martha Tibbetts. This portrait of Adele was taken five years before their marriage. The couple celebrated their 50th wedding anniversary in 1949.

Family reunions were popular. In 1926, the descendants of Edmund Jennings and Joseph Morehouse, two of Ballston's founding fathers, gathered. They are, from left to right, as follows: (first row) Alene Harriet Jennings, ? Jennings, Malcolm Leslie Jennings, Mary Baxter Jackson, Beatrice Antoinette Jennings, Lucy Fuller, Sylvia Belle Fuller, and Myra Fuller; (second row) Gladys Coon Jennings (mother of Chester Jennings), Emily Weed Smith with son William, Guy Smith, Marshall Lemet Jennings (father of Chester Jennings), Robert Miller Weed, Howard Andrew Weed, and Egbert Lockrow; (third row) Gertrude Lockrow Moncton, Ed Post, Grace Post, Viola Seelye, Mary Jennings Salzer with son Alan, Helen Merchant with Robert Salzer, Hattie Meora Morehouse Jennings holding Chester Atwood Jennings, Bert Lockrow, Franklin Weed, Grace Morehouse Weed, and Elizabeth Merchant Lockrow; (fourth row) Frances Moncton, Lawrence Treible, Julia Post Treible, Agnes Stewart Marks, George Jackson, Clara Jennings Jackson, Harold Atwood Jennings, Nellie Elizabeth Jennings, Doris Coon Jennings, Bessie Morehouse Stewart, and Roger Post; (back row) Ruth Merchant Center, Mary Adelaide Weed, Ruth Bailey Frosch, Edith VanVorst Merchant, Charles Gilpen Jennings, Laura Merchant Cunningham, and Marjorie Merchant Palmer.

The Jennings-Morehouse reunion was held at the house of Charles Platt Jennings, which is on the northeast corner of Charlton Road and Goode Street. Uriah Gregory, another founding father and Revolutionary War patriot, lived here.

Burnt Hills, NY
October 24, 1930

My dearest Edna,
You see I have gone one better than the one you addressed to me. If I over step, let me know and will try to keep within the bounds next time.

If the future looks as bright to you as it does to me, then you can understand how one wants to express himself in the most endearing terms when the one you are writing to has made that condition possible. I also want to say that you are the only woman in the world that I have been interested in for some time. If you had turned me down, life would not have been the same. You will never regret the step you have taken, while it will be a great change in your mode of living.

I intended to write sooner, but Mr. Schauber came over and [staid] late. Been getting in the apples, the call for them has been slow. It has been very cold. I sorted apples with a heavy overcoat on. I have a desire to go South again, more so now that I will have my chosen companion with me. It all depends on your wishes and how much money you want us to spend.

I trust Mr. Manchester has been informed of your resignation. Send letters addressed to me to Scotia in care of B and G.

Your fiance,

Frank

[Author's note-apparently Edna agreed to marry Frank during her annual summer visit home in August of 1930. It has been said that she agreed to marry him only if he had a full bin of coal in the cellar.]

First row, Mr. Ross G. Cunningham, Mr. Ralph H. Frankland, President, Mr. Albert V. Bigwood, Mr. Edgar I. Schauber, clerk.
Second row, Mr. Francis L. Stevens, Mr. Arthur C. Mengel, Mr. Axel R. Frieberg.

The 1948 Board of Education met at the school. Edgar Schauber raised fruit trees on his farm on Schauber Road.

106

The main portion of the Schauber house was built in 1806 by David Schauber. Family tradition holds that Native Americans answered the dinner bell and were fed with no protest from the family.

The Ashdown Oil Company conducted business from the Schauber farm. Seated on the left is Stan Ashdown, who started the company in 1933, when he sold kerosene by the bucket. In 1943, he was joined by Ray Ashdown, pictured on the right. Ray was married to Mary Schauber Ashdown.

Burnt Hills, NY
November 9, 1930

Dearest Edna,

These two words mean to me just what they imply. I trust they always will until death do us part. It was mighty nice of you to send me two letters in one week. They are the bright spots in my life.

Still selling the apples. Will have nearly 300 barrels when done, but not much money. How will it be to marry a dirt farmer and listen to farm talk? I do have a full supply of ice, meat and coal for the winter months. I attended two funerals this week. Both burials were in Hillside.

You say you are worried about your cooking. You have to exist, don't you? If you can live on it, so can I. I am not very hard to cook for. One good meal a day is good enough for me. You are smart enough to learn. My mother was a school teacher, and she was a good cook too. You said you were reluctant to give up your salary. We will make the best of it for better or for worse. I know I will be getting the better bargain. What you see in an old duffer like me, I cannot imagine. Will be at your place Nov. 26 or 27. I am counting the days. I think of you day and night, have for four and one-half years. How about that? Then we can discuss plans and business matters. I prefer to stay in your apartment and don't care to be very conspicuous. Stock up and have a pie.

I was invited down to Smith's one evening with Mr. and Mrs. Bailey. Good dinner, even if it was gotten up by a school teacher. You will say I have spread it thickly this time, rather mushy. I am saving my new suit for the special event.

From your dearly beloved,

F.B. Coons

Levinus Lansing sits in his carriage in front of his house in 1880. He was a veteran of the Civil War and ran a slaughterhouse. He willed his house to his step-son, Fred Higgins, in 1920.

The first burial in Hillside Cemetery took place in 1793. Here rests the family of Joe Bettys, a spy for the British in the Revolutionary War. His father ran a tavern at 924 Saratoga Road. He died in 1804, at the age of 88. Joe Bettys was hanged for treason in Albany in 1782.

If Edna and Frank were hungry, they could go to the Burnt Hills Diner, shown here on the right. The shoe store is on the left with the garden shop in front. Fireman's pond is in the back. Veeder & Yelverton drugstore is on the far right. It opened in 1954.

Dearest Edna,

It has been such a long time since I saw you. Maybe we could send $100.00 to see each other. I just lost a cow worth more than that, so I feel poorer. We have been selling apples here from the farm as I put an ad in the paper. People have been coming in cars, so we have been busy waiting on them. I had dinner with Dr. Kathan in Schenectady. He was the first one I told. You will have two good friends in the Coons family and enjoy them very much.

I understand a young fellow went through the ice on the lake today. He was not from here. It is such a beauty in the summer time, and can be so ugly in the winter. The boy probably didn't know the ice was not safe. Remember our stroll there last August? I so enjoyed the evening, bugs and all. I thought I walked very well that time and will again.

Has the secret leaked out yet? What about the Ketchums? If so, what did they say.

From your old friend and now your fiancee,

Frank

[Author's note-Carrie Coons, daughter of Frank's oldest half-brother, Solyman, married Dr. Dudley Kathan in 1901.]

Ballston Lake from Causeway,
Ballston, N. Y.

The causeway spanned the southern portion of the lake. It was used for a leisurely stroll and a short-cut for schoolchildren.

Courting couples enjoyed an evening stroll on the walkway, which was on the west side of Ballston Lake. One young lady complained to her escort that bugs were bothersome, but she was thrilled that he found an arrowhead for her.

The advent of power-driven boats brought new recreation to the lake. Caring for a mahogany boat can be difficult. Some camps built boathouses to protect them from the weather.

Dearest Edna,

This makes two to your one. Perhaps I am writing too often. Just imagine, next week we will see each other. I have my reservation for the train. I wonder who I will meet on this trip.

Two rainy days in succession. We have been drawing water. Enough for the house, but that is it. It is the first time the barn well has given out.

In regard to having the Robsons take your house, write to her that you have made other plans since you made her the offer. Do not tell her what plans you have made, as she will not keep it to herself. Mr. Robson is in a mess with his partner. He thinks every one is as honest as he is. Other than that, it is business as usual in Burnt Hills. We have had our moving day, so people are settled for the winter now. I see another year has gone by with no celebration of Constitution Day. People are more preoccupied now. I now have all my winter stocks- a full bin of coal and pantry full of food.

I see you have put me off another day in Columbus. Will have to stay longer, so I can see you at night. Was pleased that you like my letter. I did better than you thought I was capable of. Will close for now as Amelia is leaving and will mail it from Schenectady.

From your lonesome lover,

F.B. Coons

This two-room schoolhouse was District #1. It closed when the new school was built in 1916. After the Johnson store fire, Nathan Seelye moved his store and the post office to this building. Nathan was a local hero, having captured a horse thief who had stolen a steed from the VanVorst farm.

Nora and Earl Smith opened their grocery store in 1932. The post office was moved to Smith's Store in 1933, and yes, stamps were 2¢.

Albert Smith tends the store with Earl and Nora behind the counter in 1938. When there was a birth in Burnt Hills, Earl placed a card with the announcement on his cash register. After a bit, he would mail the card to the parents. The post office boxes can be seen on the back wall.

Dearest One,

You did the proper thing to move the date of our next meeting. Now, we will have our first Thanksgiving together. How will that seem to you?

Mrs. Robson told Amelia that they were going to stay in the Edna Davis house. She has told several others the same thing. She has been waiting for you to send her the key. She has told others that she looks forward to living next door to the Ryders. They thought that when your mother died, we would get married. Since nothing happened, they thought they figured it out wrong and think we are just running around together for a good time.

I will go to Schenectady tomorrow to get reservations for the train Tuesday night, and we can have breakfast together on Wednesday. I so look forward to seeing you.
From you loving husband to be,

FBC

Connie Falconer stands with her daughter Lela in 1964. The Riders were next-door neighbors. Their house was built c. 1840. Harold and Beulah Rider were married in 1897 and raised their nine children at this house.

The Rider family posed for this photograph. They are, from left to right, as follows: (front row) Mary Belle (face out of the picture), Marcia, Mother, Grace, and Jeanne; (back row) Doug, Mac, Clarence, Lester, and Arthur. When the children were small, they had pillow fights in the barn, when burlap bags were filled with rotten tomatoes and squash.

The interior of the Schenectady Railroad Station had stone walls, wooden benches, and globe lamps. The sound of the station master's announcements echoed through the waiting room. This is where Frank would meet Edna's train.

Dearest Edna,

Arrived in Schenectady about 1 o'clock and called home. Learned that Amelia was on Brandywine Avenue collecting rents. She was informed that I was at the depot and came to get me. My ailment is 50% better than yesterday. Have walked around here and the school buildings. As to the other matter you called my attention to, I will work on it to improve. Whenever I walk around our modern school facility, I marvel at the progress compared to the old system of one and two room houses.

We had quite an incident here with the trolley. It made the newspapers. It seems that a few head of cattle blocked the tracks, causing quite the stir. The cows were removed and no one was hurt, except those who were delayed.

The well drillers were here. They do not have to go deeper and assure me of 198 gallons per hour. The paper tonight said there were two Burnt Hills girls missing, but they have been found in Schenectady visiting a married friend.

I wish to extend to you a most heartfelt thanks for the delightful time you gave me at your apartment.

From you best friend,

FBC

The trolley stop at Forest Park was the first one north after the stop in the village of Ballston Lake. It was called the Hemlock Stop.

The trolley tracks had to be cut through "shale hill." The metal from the rails and power poles was taken to support the World War II war effort. The present-day bike path is paved on the old trolley bed.

Pamela Lacy stands on the bike path in front of the remains of the trolley power station. In this building, employees monitored generators, which provided current to the trolley cars.

Darling One,

How does that appeal to you? Your letter was received this morning and was a comfort to hear from my sweet-heart. I thought perhaps after being at home for five days, you had the opportunity to know more about me and look me over, I wondered if I had made a good impression. I did not try to put on and was my natural self outside of my affliction of walking. So I was overjoyed at your expression of love. I hope nothing will ever come between us to change your mind or mine either. When the news leaks out, what a time they will have. I think you will be happy in Burnt Hills. We will have good neighbors and friends.

Dorothy is now playing basketball. It will be good for her to exercise. Last Thursday I went with Mr. Denty and Mr. Smith to Syracuse to attend a meeting of various boards of education. Talked to one of the speakers, who was a lady. Please don't be jealous. We were the first district in the state to vote for a central, rural school. One other district received their charter one day before ours. That was the winter of 1924-1925.

We may have a radio some day, if we have the money. I don't expect the old piano will go far toward one though.

I went to the doctor's and was thoroughly examined. He said he could straighten me out in a short time. He said it was neuralgia and gave me liniment. The shoulder was more of a habit than anything else.

I spelled a word wrong in my last letter. Did you detect it? Amelia tells me they intend on sending you a Christmas present. Have been to the doctor's. Dr. Kathan and Alice Slover will make a new man of me. Alice is to give me electric treatments twice a week. I had one yesterday. It was the first time I had a spinster working over me. We are both passed the blushing stage. Now, if this letter does not match up to the others in expressing my feelings, read the others over again.

From the one who loves you most,

Frank

One of Frank's "good neighbors and friends" was George Shorey, an artist, violinist, and playwright. His plays were presented at the Calvary Episcopal Fellowship Hall.

George's first artist studio burned. It was rebuilt on the same foundation *c.* 1914. This image portrays his original studio.

This etching was done by George Shorey. It is entitled *Meadows and Gardens are Refreshed by the Snow*. He once exhibited with Grandma Moses in Hoosic Falls.

My dear one,

Seven weeks from now, I will be having the time of my life in Florida. I am glad you liked the flowers I sent.

Have sent out all my holiday cards and have received quite a few. You will have a busy Christmas. Don't eat too much. Remember the 150 limit. Amelia has the presents bought. Too many, but times have changed. I will, as usual give cash, but this year, I may give each of my people mittens too.

Enclosed you will find the names and addresses for our announcement. We are missing so much by being apart. The thrills two people get when fond of each other are so important, especially before the ceremony. Amelia went to the city's clerk today to ask about the license. She was told we could get on there and be married right after. Saw Mr. Bailey. He asked if I was going to be married. He said he would not blame me and put my feet under my own table. I got my hair cut the other day your way, so you can see I obey very well.

You will never regret that step taken. Now I write of our upcoming event. I prefer to have a quiet affair in Schenectady. I would like your Aunt Mary to come if it is not too cold. We have an apartment rented in Florida. It is $35.00 a week.

Don't look at the stock market report. Poor reading. Have been reading a book, The Seed. I would not want Dorothy to read it. It is about birth control. At your age it would be all right to read, better to be informed.

Your ardent lover,

FBC

PS. Did you wear the ring? Don't be ashamed of it for the quality is there if not the size.

The Woodside Knitting Mill was located at 883 Saratoga Road. In this early 1930 photograph, Sibyl Larkin, office manager, stands in the middle of the shop. Charles Manzer, Frank Meacham, and Joseph Ouellette are also pictured. They made children's sweaters and mittens.

Nine

1931

"The Witch"—every town has at least one!

My dearest Edna,

What changes the year 1931 will bring to both of us, lets hope it will be happy. It is up to each of us that no friction occurs, so I wish you a happy New Year.

If the list of announcements is too long, the one to my aunt, Mrs. H. Hamilton could be eliminated as she lives with my cousin, Jennie. The names you asked for are Mrs. Margaret Abbs and Mr. and Mrs. Vagg. As for our home coming, it should be about the first week in April. Do you wish me to resign from the board of education? School matters take a great deal of my time. Are you the one to engage a preacher or should I? The reservations for the train out of New York City should be secured soon. How much do you think we should spend on our trip? We should get a compartment on the train so we can be alone and by ourselves.

Mrs. Wesson is just alive. What will Ashley do than?

Did not quite get your full meaning in regard to being a nurse and housekeeper combined. Those people can be hired, but love and companionship cannot. I am invited to play cards at two of our teachers, Miss Chatfield and Miss Murray. I don't expect to win. This week I went to see Eddie Cantor in the movies. I think he is one of the best. I see that I am writing uphill. It is said that one who does, will be rich. Mr. Upham asked George Bates for your address. I could have given it to him, but did not let on. That's all we need now.

Goodbye for now, my dear. If I don't hear from you soon, I will wire or telephone. This is not much of a love letter. You can see that my heart is in the right place.

Lovingly yours,
Frank

Author's note: Mrs. Wesson was Ashley Baker's housekeeper.

Sibyl Curtis and George Bates stand in front of their home at 868 Saratoga Road. George was a town councilman, tax collector, member of the board of education, and a charter member of the Rotary Club. They were the parents of Carlton and Dorothy.

George Bates's retirement house was at 194 Kingsley Road. It was previously owned by Evlia Wair.

Sibyl Curtis Bates's brother was Kent Curtis, who owned the lumber mill. He stands here with wife, Lucy. Their children are Bob, Doris, Nancy, Lucille, and Mary Lou.

Friday afternoon

Dearest Edna,

Went down to Dr. Bomback and made arrangements with him to officiate. St. George's is open all the time and they do not charge for the use of the church. As to Rob and Edith, do you intend to send them word at all? If you don't, the public will have a lot to talk about. Talked to Lieut. Bailey today. You can depend on him. He said he could never live alone as he likes the companionship of ladies. There is never a scandal about him. Just received your letter. Do take it easy. It would not be good if either of us got sick now. We have been busy with school matters, and I believe we have a fine teaching staff for the coming year. I am told by those who should know, that Antoinette has been spending time with Ashley again. That may take some of the heat off of us when news gets out.

Amelia was asking what she should give you as a present. She wanted to know if you had a coffee percolator. I am somewhat better in the leg. I will take a cane on the trip as you requested. Now don't wonder about what you have done. Let us live for the future. I have made our train reservations. At first, all we could get was upper berths, but I insisted, and got, a compartment. I did not put in as much ice as last year as you said you would use your refrigerator.

As for the plays in New York City, I understand "Green Pastures" is having a good run. High noon would be a good time for our event in Schenectady. I do not want to be at the depot too long to make a show of ourselves. I have high hopes for our future here in Burnt Hills. I am sure you will make good friends and enjoy our peaceful village.

To the dearest woman on earth with kisses thrown in.

FBC

Top row: Francis L. Stevens, assistant principal & science teacher; Marcia Chatfield, history; Ray H. Smith, principal; Margaret Dadez, secretary; Mrs. Gertrude Maess, homemaking; Arthur Hammalainen, Jr. High history & civics.

Middle Row: Gertrude Rice, 4th grade; Edith Livingston, 3rd grade; Doris Bishop, Jr. High English; Mr. Whitney, shop; Ethel McChesney, Jr. High math; Frances Mangan, languages; Marjory Keck, 5th grade.

Bottom row: Mrs. Bessie Brown, math; Florence Lees, 2nd grade; Mary A'Hearn, High School English; Ruth Murray, 6th grade; Mrs. Ray H. Smith, 1st grade; and Gertrude B. Nash, music.

The teaching staff of the BH-BL Central School posed for this photograph in 1931.

Antoinette Seelye married Ashley Baker in 1932. They are photographed in the front parlor of the Seelye home. Gilbert is in the background.

Edna did make good friends. Three of her bridge partners and traveling companions were, from left to right, Betty Seelye, Audrey Laws, and Maude Mengel.

Dearest Edna,

I have not heard a word about the rumor. If it was going around, Mr. Young would tell me as he is up to the barber shop often and gets all the gossip.

I don't know if I told you about attending Miss Wesson's funeral. The new rector officiated. He is not a bad looking man, a good speaker as most Episcopalians are. Dorothy had a new coat that her Grandmother sent her. It has fur on the collar and cuffs. Quite good looking.

My things will all be ready to be taken up to your house. I was intending on keeping my den and desk here, but they need the room. We can get very good bargains on 1929 cars. I will trade the old one in. The new models are easier to drive, when you learn to do so. That will settle matters with my people. They have been here twelve years and we have done well to get along so well. These are my plans. If you do not agree, let me know. You are the boss. 11:45 wedding at St. George's. Have Amelia and Riley there and Rob and Edith and maybe your Aunt Mary. After the wedding, make out my will and have it executed in front of a notary. Then take the 12:57 train to New York and get our dinner on the train. Will arrive in New York about 5 PM, then to the hotel for supper. Then to the theater. After the theater, to OUR room. The next morning, take the train to Florida. You told me to look as young as I can, and I tell you to look as old as you can. Don't cover up any gray hairs.

Don't fail to arrive on Wednesday. If we have time, I will take you up to see your Aunt Mary. Should I take two or three suits? Will you have any room in the trunk? Probably not.

Lovingly,

Frank

Author's note: Frank and Edna were married on Thursday, February 5, 1931.

A picture of Frank and Edna's wedding has not been found. Other weddings represent them. Sibyl Curtis married George Bates on September 11, 1920, in a garden wedding at her home. She is pictured with her sister Elizabeth.

Phillis Laws married Walter Brandt on November 24, 1951. The wedding party consisted of, from left to right, Frank Coons Jr., Willis Currier, Van Gifford, Lee Carlton, Henry Howard, Walt and Phil, June Carlton, Anna Smith, Mary Elizabeth Seelye, Shirley Brandt, and Phyllis Crowley. Edna attended this wedding.

On August 23, 1934, Anita Egan married Fred Wagner at Our Lady of Grace Church in Ballston Lake. From left to right are Al Tiller, Dorothy Egan, the bride, and the groom.

Edna Coons (left) traveled to Mexico in 1947. She was photographed there with Mrs. Alice Merchant. Edna kept a detailed travel log, and like her late husband, accounted for every expense, including 25¢ for postcards.

Epilogue

Frank and Edna sent out their wedding announcements along with a card stating, "At home, May 1st." They settled into married life in Burnt Hills. The couple had 14 happy years together until Frank's death in 1945. Edna bought a copy of *Fanny Farmer's Cook Book* and followed recipes to the letter. She did make one well-known blooper when she presented a cooked, albeit rancid, turkey for a church supper. "Brick" Falconer saved the day by buying one from a local restaurant known as the Green Lantern.

Edna and Frank planted fruit trees and bushes and tended the gardens at 97 Lakehill Road. Edna did complain when Gilbert Seelye's cows crossed the road and ate her tulips.

Frank continued to keep meticulous records of his finances and owned several rental properties in Burnt Hills and Schenectady. He was generous with Edna, buying her clothing and household items. He was also generous with his grandchildren; however, his gifts were always practical. Frank continued to serve on the board of education and was a vestryman at the Calvary Episcopal Church, while Edna served as president of Saint Mary's Guild there.

Edna enjoyed playing bridge with her friends. She presented herself as stern and proper, but is recalled by some as warm and fun-loving within her own circle. During her 28 years as a resident of Burnt Hills, she accomplished much in improving the community life. She was a prime force in the formation of the Burnt Hills-Ballston Lake Community Library and the Women's Club.

After Frank's death, Edna continued to manage his investments and traveled extensively. She bought a new Buick each year. When she and her friends traveled, they always took Edna's car. Once, the ladies got lost in Nova Scotia. Edna saved the day, as she could speak fluent French.

Edna witnessed changes in Ballston, such as the building of the BH-BL High School in 1955. Also, Burnt Hills was gradually changing from a farming community to suburbia. Her husband's old farm at 73 Lakehill Road became the Townley Drive housing development. While all this was occurring, Edna preserved her letters from Frank, having tied them together with a pink satin ribbon. He once wrote to her that he would like to get her letters published in a book. It is ironic that 70 years later, it would be his letters that are published.

A parting thought . . . A wise lady once said, "Gossip is like rocking in a chair. It gives you something to do, but it gets you nowhere."